For Laura and Tom

moro easy

Sam and Sam Clark

Photography by Susan Bell

EBURY
PRESS

contents

introduction   9

easy toasts   **15**

easy eggs and dairy   **37**

easy salads   **77**

easy veg   **101**

easy rice, grains and pulses   **141**

easy fish   **167**

easy meat   **215**

easy one-pot   **247**

easy desserts   **275**

suppliers   **303**

index   **307**

about the authors   **314**

acknowledgements   **318**

introduction

introduction

That COVID moment in 2020 when we were forced to shut the doors to Moro was profound and surreal. That space we so associated with our lives, energy and laughter just echoed with uncertainty. Schools and universities closed. The house filled up and there we were, like much of the world, desperately adapting. Surprisingly quickly, spring and then summer came to the rescue! It was impossible not to feel positive. Without traffic or aeroplanes, the bird song was intense, and blossoms and blue sky prevailed. For once we had time to look up to the sky and really breathe. Life had changed. We were able to read, garden and still have time to eavesdrop on the homeschooling before organising lunch. The cooking was a big thing.

THE COOKING WAS A BIG THING. Not in a horrible way, nevertheless, five people with healthy appetites under one roof, 24/7. Unlike a typical household, there were two extreme food lovers, poised to do their thing. We had time to reconnect with our culinary urges. We still love cooking (thank the stars!) but didn't want to spend more time on it than was absolutely necessary.

The task of documenting the simple recipes that we cooked during lockdown was immensely rewarding. To make Moro accessible, with the home cook at the forefront of our minds, required a different discipline with not too many ingredients and uncomplicated methods. The photographs for the book were mostly shot in Spain, at our home nestled between Seville and Cordoba, on the edge of the Sierra Norte. This also marked a special moment as it was the first time we had travelled since lockdown. We had bought the shell of a ruin ten years before, but the quote to renovate it was beyond our means, so we left it. The walls continued to crumble, and the roof caved in until the town hall threatened to repossess it. This spurred us on to begin the restoration and after two years we were just beginning to enjoy the house when COVID shut it down again; we returned for the first time in February 2022. It felt right, a celebration of life beginning again, and to mark this occasion and our 25th anniversary at Moro, *Moro Easy* was created.

easy toasts

The Spanish word for toast is *tostada*. A *montadito* is bread or toast with a topping, tapas on toast! Try to serve a varied selection of these for pre-dinner nibbles or a light bite with drinks; fresh, dry fino or manzanilla sherry is the perfect partner. Some of the toasts will benefit from being warm, as indicated.

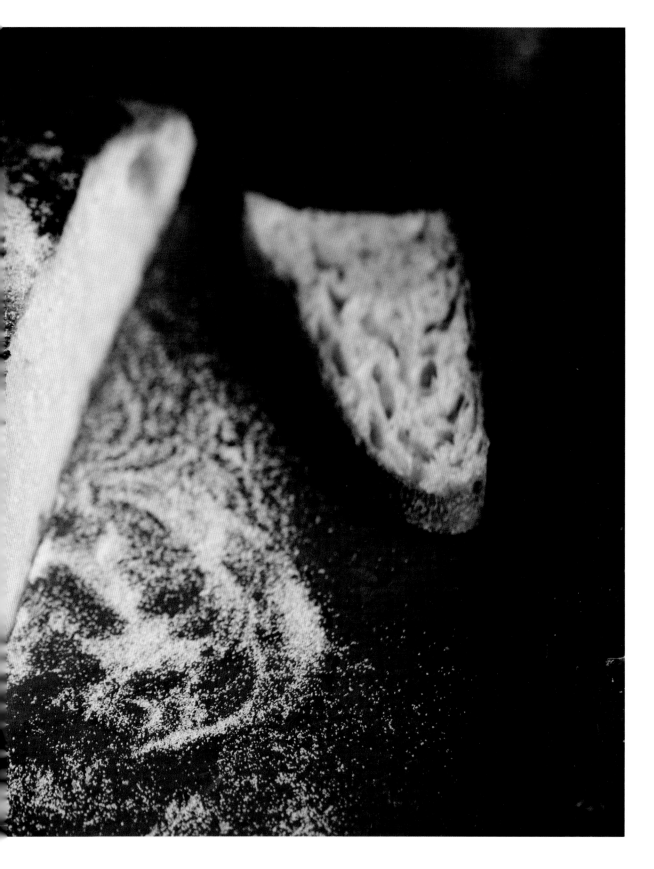

pepper, anchovy and chopped egg

The marriage of the sweet peppers, salty anchovies and creamy egg make this toast a visual and taste sensation. Serves 4

6–8 roasted piquillo peppers, from a jar (page 303), or 2 romano peppers (180g), roasted until soft, then peeled and deseeded
½ tablespoon good-quality red wine vinegar + pinch sugar if not sweet
4 tablespoons extra virgin olive oil
8 slices sourdough or 4 slices ciabatta (if ciabatta, use slices 8cm wide, cut in half horizontally)
½ garlic clove
1 organic or free-range egg, hard-boiled and finely chopped
8 best-quality anchovy fillets in olive oil (we use Ortiz, page 304)
2 tablespoons finely chopped flat-leaf parsley

Cut the peppers into strips and mix with the vinegar, olive oil, salt and pepper.

Toast the bread, brush the cut side of the garlic over the hot toast, then spoon the peppers on top, followed by the chopped egg and anchovy fillets. Finish with the chopped parsley.

tomato, avocado and anchovy

Sourcing good-quality anchovies is important. The best come from the Cantabrian coast and Bay of Biscay, like Ortiz, Santona or Don Bocarte. You can easily source these online or in good delis. Serves 4

4 large ripe tomatoes (200g), coarsely grated
½ teaspoon thyme leaves (optional)
4 tablespoons extra virgin olive oil
½ garlic clove, crushed with a little salt
8 slices sourdough or 4 slices ciabatta (if ciabatta, use slices 8cm wide, cut in half horizontally)
1 avocado, sliced
8 best-quality anchovy fillets in olive oil (we use Ortiz, page 304)

Mix the tomatoes, thyme (if using), olive oil and garlic together and check for seasoning.

Toast the bread, spoon the tomatoes on top, followed by the avocado and anchovy fillets.

chorizo, tomato and chilli

Tomato toast but with chorizo and chilli. Make sure the chorizo is hot. Serves 4

4 large ripe tomatoes (200g), coarsely grated
4 tablespoons extra virgin olive oil
½ garlic clove, crushed with a little salt
4 cooking chorizo (150–200g), cut into quarters lengthways
8 slices sourdough or 4 slices ciabatta (if ciabatta, use slices 8cm wide, cut in half horizontally)
2 tablespoons finely chopped fresh or pickled green chillies

Mix the grated tomatoes with 2 tablespoons olive oil and the garlic and check for seasoning.

Heat a frying pan over a medium heat, add the rest of the olive oil and cook the chorizo on both sides, until slightly crisp and caramelised.

Toast the bread, spoon the tomatoes on top, followed by the chorizo, and sprinkle over the chilli.

tomato and jamón

Pan con tomate is the classic Spanish toast for breakfast, and tomato toast with jamón a close second. If you can buy the superior jamón ibérico, it is worth it. For a vegetarian alternative, replace the jamón with a line of finely chopped black or green olives (50g) down the middle of the toast. Serves 4

4 large ripe tomatoes (200g), coarsely grated
4 tablespoons extra virgin olive oil
½ garlic clove, crushed with a little salt
8 slices sourdough or 4 slices ciabatta (if ciabatta, use slices 8cm wide, cut in half horizontally)
8 small slices (80g) jamón ibérico or jamón serrano (page 303) or 50g finely chopped black or green olives

Combine the tomatoes, olive oil and garlic and check for seasoning.

Toast the bread and spoon the tomatoes on top, followed by the jamón (or olives) in a line.

tortilla, green pepper and alioli

We first ate this in Barcelona's Boqueria Market many years ago.
The secret is a thin tortilla, barely 2cm thick. It is the ideal breakfast
sandwich. This is particularly delicious when the tortilla is still warm.
Alioli is garlic mayonnaise. You could double the quantity and keep
extra in the fridge. We always add the garlic prior to eating, otherwise
the flavour of the garlic can taste stale. Serves 4

4 tablespoons olive oil
1 banana shallot (60g), finely sliced
150g potatoes, peeled, cut into quarters, very thinly sliced and lightly salted
2 large organic or free-range eggs
8 slices sourdough or 4 slices ciabatta (if ciabatta, use slices 8cm wide,
   cut in half horizontally)
4-6 tablespoons alioli (see below)
2 green bell peppers, roasted until soft, peeled, deseeded and sliced
   into thin strips

Alioli
1 large organic or free-range egg yolk
½ garlic clove, crushed to a smooth paste with ½ teaspoon salt
1 tablespoon lemon juice
1 teaspoon Dijon mustard
250ml sunflower oil

Make the alioli. Whisk together the egg yolk, garlic, lemon juice and
mustard in a medium bowl. Whisking constantly, slowly drizzle in the oil,
drop by drop at first, until all the oil has been incorporated and the alioli
is thick and smooth. Check for seasoning. If too thick, thin with a few drops
of water or lemon juice.

For the tortilla, add 2 tablespoons olive oil to a small non-stick frying pan
over a medium heat. Once hot, but not smoking, add the shallot and a pinch
of salt. Fry over a medium heat for 5-7 minutes until soft and lightly golden.
Add the potatoes and fry for 10 minutes, stirring regularly, until tender.

Whisk the eggs in a bowl. Transfer the potato/onion mixture to the eggs,
stir well, and check for seasoning.

Turn the heat up to high and add the remaining 2 tablespoons olive oil
to the pan. Once very hot, add the egg mixture and lightly shake the pan
to spread out evenly. Fry for 30 seconds to 1 minute until golden on the
underside, then flip onto a plate and slide back into the pan for another
20 seconds until just set. Transfer to a plate.

Toast the bread, spread a generous amount of alioli over the toasts, and place a wedge of tortilla (ideally warm) on top, followed by the peppers.

Pictured on page 23

courgette, mint and jamón

Slow-cooked sweet courgettes go so well with the salty jamón and mint. Chopped olives instead of jamón are a fine vegetarian substitute. Serve slightly warm. Serves 4

4 tablespoons olive oil + extra to drizzle
600g courgettes, trimmed, thinly sliced and lightly salted
2 tablespoons mint leaves, finely chopped
2 tablespoons pine nuts, lightly toasted
8 slices sourdough or 4 slices ciabatta (if ciabatta, use slices 8cm wide,
   cut in half horizontally)
1 garlic clove, cut in half
8 small slices (80g) jamón ibérico or jamón serrano (page 303)
   or 50g finely chopped black or green olives

Heat the olive oil in a large frying pan over a medium heat. Add the courgettes, salt and pepper and cook for 10-15 minutes, stirring occasionally, until they are very soft and sweet. Add the mint and pine nuts and check for seasoning.

Toast the bread and rub lightly with the cut garlic clove. Spoon the courgettes over the toast and lay the jamón on top (or place the olives in a line). Drizzle with a little extra olive oil to finish.

crab, Oloroso sherry and alioli

As well as dry sherry, crab and other *mariscos* (shellfish) go so well with an oxidised sherry like an Oloroso, particularly the sweet brown meat of the crab. The toast is lifted with the chilli and thyme. Serve at room temperature or slightly warm. Serves 4

50g butter
3 spring onions (white and green parts), thinly sliced
2 heaped teaspoons thyme leaves (lemon thyme if possible)
75ml Oloroso dulce (sweet Oloroso sherry)
300g crab meat (200g white + 100g brown meat), or 200g brown shrimps
8 slices sourdough or 4 slices ciabatta (if ciabatta, use slices 8cm wide,
   cut in half horizontally)
4 tablespoons alioli (page 24)
1 long red chilli, finely chopped

Melt the butter in a saucepan over a medium heat, and when it foams add the spring onions and two thirds of the thyme leaves. Season with a little salt and fry for 4-5 minutes, stirring occasionally, until soft and sweet.

Add the sherry, simmer for a couple of minutes to burn off the alcohol, then stir in the crab or shrimps and warm through. Remove from the heat, check for seasoning and set aside.

Toast the bread, then spread ½ tablespoon of alioli on each toast, followed by the crab (or shrimps). Serve immediately, with the chopped chilli and remaining thyme on top.

goat's cheese and roasted red onions

No surprises here, but warm the red onions (and goat's cheese) through prior to serving. Serves 4

4 red onions, cut into wedges 2cm thick at the widest point
3 tablespoons olive oil
2 heaped teaspoons finely chopped rosemary
1 tablespoon good-quality red wine vinegar + pinch sugar if not sweet
8 slices sourdough or 4 slices ciabatta (if ciabatta, use slices 8cm wide,
  cut in half horizontally)
250–300g soft goat's cheese
2 tablespoons pine nuts, lightly toasted
1 teaspoon fresh mint, chopped

Preheat the oven to 200°C/400°F/gas 6.

Place the onions, olive oil, rosemary and vinegar in a mixing bowl, season with salt and pepper, and toss well. Spread on a roasting tray and roast for 25–30 minutes, stirring once or twice, until sweet, soft and caramelised. Remove from the oven and leave to cool slightly.

Toast the bread, then spread the soft goat's cheese liberally on top, a layer about 0.5cm thick. Spoon the warm onions on top and sprinkle with the pine nuts and the mint.

Pictured on page 31

serranito – pork, green pepper and jamón

Another winning combination that is big on flavour and a substantial bite. Serve hot or warm. Serves 4

4 large ripe tomatoes (200g), coarsely grated
3 tablespoons olive oil + extra to drizzle
½ garlic clove, crushed with a little salt
160g pork fillet, cut into 8 slices 5mm thick and rubbed with a little olive oil
1 teaspoon fennel seeds (optional)
8 slices sourdough or 4 slices ciabatta (if ciabatta, use slices 8cm wide, cut in half horizontally)
24 Padrón peppers, fried until soft, or 2 green bell peppers, roasted until soft, peeled, deseeded and sliced into thin strips
8 small slices (80g) jamón ibérico or jamón serrano (page 303)

Mix the grated tomato with 2 tablespoons olive oil and garlic, check for seasoning and set aside.

Place a frying pan over a medium to high heat, and when hot add the remaining tablespoon of olive oil. Season the pork with salt, pepper and the fennel seeds (if using), and fry for a minute on either side, until just cooked through.

Toast the bread and spoon over the tomatoes, followed by the pork, peppers and jamón. Serve immediately.

prego – steak, red wine and onions

Red onions cooked in red wine on top of a thin minute steak that has been seared in the pan. The Portuguese often choose it at the end of a meal. Serve hot or warm. Serves 4

50g butter
2 tablespoons olive oil
3 red onions (300g), sliced
2 teaspoons thyme leaves
250ml red wine
2 sirloin/rib-eye steaks (400g in total)
8 slices sourdough or 4 slices ciabatta (if ciabatta, use slices 8cm wide, cut in half horizontally)

Place a frying pan over a medium heat, and add the butter and 1 tablespoon olive oil. When the butter foams, add the onions, thyme leaves and a pinch of salt then gently fry for 12–15 minutes, stirring occasionally, until soft and caramelised. Add the wine and simmer for a few minutes until the wine has reduced and formed a sauce with the onions. Check for seasoning, then set aside and keep warm.

Clean the pan and return it to a high heat. Rub the other tablespoon of olive oil over the steaks and season with salt and pepper. When the pan is smoking hot, add the steaks and sear for a couple of minutes on either side (4–6 minutes in total for medium rare). Remove from the heat and leave to rest for 5–10 minutes. Discard the fat and slice the steak. Add any steak juices to the red wine sauce and warm through.

Toast the bread, spoon the steak and onions on top and serve immediately.

easy eggs
and dairy

Eggs are so versatile, quick and easy, it was important to include lots of recipes to be enjoyed at any time of day. The spiced potato cake (page 104) goes well with all of the egg recipes in this chapter.

Labneh is strained yoghurt and is similar to fresh cheese in texture and flavour. Combining cream cheese and yoghurt is a super quick way to replicate this. Then it is a question of toppings! Choose from any of the recipes here or make up your own. Be sure to spoon the topping whilst still warm or hot onto the labneh as the cool creaminess contrasts well with the heat. Flatbread or pitta is essential for scooping.

fried eggs with toasted cumin

To embellish this dish a little more, serve with *mojo verde* (page 184).
Serves 4

enough olive oil to cover the base of the frying pan with a depth of 1cm
4–8 organic or free-range eggs, cold from the fridge
2 teaspoons lightly toasted roughly ground cumin seeds
1 green chilli, deseeded and finely chopped

Place a frying pan over a medium to high heat and add the olive oil. When
the oil is hot, but not smoking, crack an egg into a cup and slide it into the
oil (maximum of 4 at one time). Take care that you are not splattered by
the hot oil. The oil should be hot enough that the edges of the white start
bubbling straightaway as it hits the pan.

Fry the eggs for 1½–2 minutes, or until the white is very crispy and golden
around the edges and puffed up around the yolk. If the edges are getting
too dark, turn the heat down slightly.

Transfer to a plate, making sure to drain any excess oil. Season liberally with
salt, cumin and chilli.

fried eggs with yoghurt
and chilli butter

Yoghurt and chilli butter is a classic Turkish combination, delicious with
a fried egg. Spinach braised with a pinch of oregano or marjoram is a
delicious addition here. Serves 4

2 tablespoons olive oil
25g butter
4 organic or free-range eggs
200g Greek yoghurt, seasoned with a little salt
1 portion of chilli butter (page 150)

Place a frying pan over a medium to high heat and add the olive oil
and butter. When the butter begins to foam, crack the eggs into the pan.
Season with salt and pepper and fry the eggs for 1½–2 minutes, or until the
white is crispy and golden around the edges and the yolk is to your liking.

Spread a large dollop of yoghurt onto four small plates, place the egg on
top, a little off-centre, and spoon over the warm chilli butter.

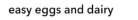

eggs with chorizo, tomato and green chilli

There is a famous restaurant in Madrid, Casa Lucio, that specialises in fried eggs over chips. It is simplicity brought to perfection. They use the best quality eggs, olive oil and potatoes and you can choose an additional topping of chorizo, jamón or *pisto* (Spanish ratatouille). Our version is lighter with fresh tomato instead of chips (we aren't stopping you!) and green chilli for a little kick. Serves 4

2 tablespoons olive oil
3 spring onions (green and white parts), finely chopped
100g green bell pepper, finely chopped
2 garlic cloves, finely chopped
100g cooking chorizo (page 304), cut into quarters lengthways,
    then into 1cm cubes
500g ripe cherry tomatoes, blitzed
4 large organic or free-range eggs
3 teaspoons finely chopped green chilli
toast, to serve

Heat the olive oil in a large frying pan over a medium heat and add the spring onions, green peppers, garlic, chorizo and a pinch of salt. Cook for 8–10 minutes, stirring occasionally, or until the vegetables and chorizo are soft and caramelised.

Add the tomatoes, bring to a gentle simmer and cook for a further 10 minutes. Check for seasoning.

Turn the heat to high so the sauce is really bubbling. Make 4 pockets and crack an egg into each pocket. Simmer (lid on for speed) until the white is set and the yolk is to your liking. Remove from the heat and rest briefly.

Sprinkle with the chilli and serve with toast.

fried eggs, peas and chorizo

Delicious with green chilli and coriander salsa (page 44). Serves 4

1 tablespoon olive oil
100g cooking chorizo (page 304), cut into quarters lengthways,
   then into 1cm cubes
1 garlic clove, chopped
250g petits pois, thawed if frozen
4 organic or free-range eggs
1 tablespoon roughly chopped flat-leaf parsley
toast, to serve

Place a large frying pan over a medium heat and add the olive oil. When the oil is hot, add the chorizo and fry for 3–5 minutes, stirring occasionally, until slightly caramelised and beginning to crisp, and the red oil from the paprika has been released.

Add the garlic, fry for 1 minute, then add the peas and continue to cook for a few more minutes, stirring occasionally, until the peas are tender.

Create 4 spaces in the peas and crack an egg into each one. Season the peas and eggs with salt and pepper. Fry for 2–4 minutes, until the white and yolk are to your liking.

Serve immediately, with the parsley sprinkled on top and toast on the side.

shakshuka with green chilli and coriander salsa

No brunch is complete without shakshuka. The green chilli and coriander salsa and Greek yoghurt (or fried halloumi) on the side make this a winner. The salsa is just fantastic with so many dishes. Make extra and keep in the fridge; it will last at least a week. Serves 4

8 tablespoons olive oil
3 banana shallots (200g), finely chopped
1–2 red romero peppers (250g), cut in half, deseeded and finely chopped
1 small green bell pepper (150g), cut in half, deseeded and finely chopped
2 teaspoons finely chopped red chilli
3 garlic cloves, finely chopped
3 heaped teaspoons ground cumin + extra for serving
½ teaspoon hot smoked paprika
600g soft ripe tomatoes
1 x 400g tin tomatoes, blitzed in a food processor
4–8 large organic or free-range eggs, depending on how hungry you are

Green chilli and coriander salsa
2 garlic cloves, crushed with salt
4 green chillies, deseeded and finely chopped
4 tablespoons finely chopped coriander
4 tablespoons olive oil
4 teaspoons lemon juice

To serve
green chilli and coriander salsa
150g Greek yoghurt or 250g halloumi, cut into 5mm slices and fried (page 74)
flatbreads or pittas, warmed

To make the shakshuka, heat the olive oil in a large frying pan over a medium heat and add the shallots, peppers, red chilli, garlic, cumin and a big pinch of salt. Stir and cook on a medium heat for 10–12 minutes, until the shallots are caramelised and sweet and the peppers are soft.

Continued on page 46

Continued from page 44

Add the paprika and all of the tomatoes, then bring to a gentle simmer and cook for a further 20-25 minutes until the sauce has thickened. Check for seasoning. This stage can be done ahead of time.

When you are ready to eat, turn the heat to high so the sauce is really bubbling. Make 4-8 pockets in the sauce and crack an egg into each pocket. Simmer for 4-5 minutes (or less with the lid on for speed) until the white is set and the yolk is to your liking. Remove from the heat and rest briefly.

To make the green chilli salsa, mix all the ingredients together and check for seasoning.

Sprinkle over a pinch of cumin and serve with the chilli and coriander salsa and Greek yoghurt (or halloumi), and warm flatbreads on the side.

Pictured on page 45

menemen - turkish eggs with spinach, tomato, feta and dill

This is on our breakfast menu at Morito Hackney Road. *Sujuk*, Turkish sausage, is optional. Serves 4

4 tablespoons olive oil
4 spring onions (white and green parts), finely chopped
½ green bell pepper, cut in half and finely chopped
3 garlic cloves, finely chopped
2 teaspoons roughly ground cumin seeds
2 heaped teaspoons roughly ground coriander seeds
¼ teaspoon smoked paprika
400g ripe vine tomatoes, diced
250g baby spinach, washed, wilted in a dry pan, drained in a colander
  and excess water squeezed out
6 tablespoons chopped dill + extra sprigs
8 large organic or free-range eggs, lightly whisked and seasoned
  with salt and pepper
80g feta, crumbled
100g *sujuk*, cut into 1cm rounds and fried (optional)
1 teaspoon Turkish chilli flakes (page 304)
toast or flatbreads, to serve

Heat the olive oil in a large frying pan over a medium heat and add the spring onions, green pepper, garlic, spices and a pinch of salt. Cook for 5 minutes, until caramelised and sweet, then add the tomatoes and simmer for 6–8 more minutes, until the tomatoes have thickened to a sauce consistency.

Add the spinach and three-quarters of the dill. Stir well and cook until wilted. Check for seasoning. This stage can be done ahead of time.

When you are ready to eat, turn the heat to high, stir in the eggs until evenly mixed and cook for 2 minutes, until cooked. Scatter over the feta and the warm *sujuk* (if using), stir once more, and check for seasoning.

Scatter the rest of the chopped dill and the extra sprigs on top and sprinkle with the chilli flakes. Serve with toast or flatbreads.

omelette with sweet herbs, feta, pine nuts and sumac

This omelette suits a lunch or light supper, with a pleasing saltiness from the feta and subtle complexity from the herbs. Serves 4

60g butter
8 organic or free-range eggs, whisked and lightly seasoned
    with salt and pepper
3 tablespoons each tarragon, dill, basil and flat-leaf parsley,
    roughly chopped + a few extra sprigs
6 tablespoons pine nuts, lightly toasted
80g feta, finely crumbled
3 teaspoons sumac
optional extras: fried courgettes or blanched asparagus

For each omelette, place a large frying pan over a medium to high heat and add 15g butter. When the butter begins to foam, pour roughly a quarter of the egg mixture into the pan and swirl it around to cover the bottom. Tilt the pan, draw one of the edges of the omelette into the middle, tilt again and allow the runny egg to run into the gap. Sprinkle over a quarter of the herbs, 1 tablespoon pine nuts, 20g feta and a pinch of sumac. Cook for a few more seconds, then roll the omelette into a fat sausage with a spatula and slide off onto a wide plate.

Repeat for the remaining three omelettes.

Serve with the rest of the herbs, pine nuts and sumac on top. If you want to add courgettes or asparagus, make sure they are hot, then place in the centre of each omelette straight after the feta, before rolling up.

Pictured on pages 52-3

labneh, asparagus, chilli butter and dukkah

Dukkah is a nut and spice blend that is Egyptian in origin and popular throughout the Middle East. We use sesame and cashews in ours, but feel free to use other combinations. Warm dukkah as a nibble with an aperitivo is delicious. This recipe makes a generous portion, but it is always good to have extra as it is so versatile and superb for enhancing the texture of a dish. You can keep it in the fridge for a week or two; just remember to warm through prior to using because of the butter. Serves 4

150g cream cheese
500g strained Greek yoghurt
16 asparagus spears, woody ends snapped off
2 tablespoons extra virgin olive oil
1 tablespoon lemon juice
1 portion chilli butter (page 150)
½ portion dukkah
2-4 flatbreads or pittas, warmed

Dukkah
50g sesame seeds
40g butter
2 rounded teaspoons ground coriander seeds
2 rounded teaspoons ground cumin seeds
80g cashews, roughly crushed
1 teaspoon hot paprika or Aleppo chilli flakes (page 304)

To make the dukkah, lightly toast the sesame seeds over a low to medium heat, stirring regularly, until they begin to colour. Transfer the seeds to a bowl and set aside.

Place the pan back on the heat and melt the butter. When it begins to foam, add the coriander and cumin, stir well for 15 seconds, then stir in the cashews and fry until golden, about 2-4 minutes. Put the sesame seeds back into the pan along with the paprika or chilli flakes. Season well with salt, then remove from the heat and leave to cool.

To make the labneh, combine the cream cheese and yoghurt, season with salt to taste and spread out on a large plate.

Boil the asparagus in salted water for 2-4 minutes, depending on the thickness of the spears. Drain the asparagus, dress with the olive oil and lemon, place on top of the labneh, spoon over the chilli butter, and sprinkle on the dukkah. Serve with warm flatbreads or pittas.

labneh, sun-dried tomato, coriander and fennel seeds

This recipe pushes the boundaries of sun-dried tomatoes, which we are perhaps a bit indifferent about nowadays. This is almost addictive. Serves 4

150g cream cheese
500g Greek yoghurt
8 tablespoons olive oil
4 garlic cloves, finely chopped
2 teaspoons coriander seeds
2 teaspoons fennel seeds
8 sun-dried tomatoes, finely chopped (we use the dehydrated ones
    and rehydrate them in a bowl of just-boiled water until soft)
1 teaspoon chilli flakes (we use Aleppo chilli flakes, page 304)
2–4 flatbreads or pittas, warmed

To make the labneh, combine the cream cheese and yoghurt, season with salt to taste and spread out on a large plate.

Put a frying pan over a medium heat and add the olive oil. When hot, but not smoking, stir in the garlic and whole spices and fry until the garlic is just golden, about 1–2 minutes. Season lightly with salt and pepper.

Add the sun-dried tomatoes and chilli flakes. Stir for 20 seconds, then remove from the heat and spoon over the labneh.

Serve immediately with warm flatbreads or pittas.

labneh, sweetcorn, coriander and paprika

Corn on the cob is best for this, but do not underestimate tinned sweetcorn. It works really well too! For more smoky complexity (and when you have more time), grill the cobs (husks on) on the barbecue. This is also delicious as a side to pork or chicken. Serves 4

2 corn on the cob or 250g tinned sweetcorn
75g butter
3 spring onions (white and green parts), finely chopped
1 garlic clove, finely chopped
1 tablespoon roughly ground coriander seeds
4 sun-dried tomatoes, finely chopped (we use the dehydrated ones
   and rehydrate them in a bowl of just-boiled water until soft)
5 tablespoons chopped coriander
½ level teaspoon hot paprika
150g cream cheese
500g strained Greek yoghurt
2-4 flatbreads or pittas, warmed

Boil the whole sweetcorn in unsalted water until tender (about 5 minutes). Or barbecue the corn in their husks for a few minutes on each side until tender and slightly charred in parts. When cool enough to handle, slice the kernels off the core.

Melt the butter in a saucepan over a medium heat and stir until it starts to caramelise (the white bits of whey will turn golden), about 3-5 minutes. Add the spring onions, garlic and coriander seeds, stir together and cook for 3 minutes over a medium heat until soft and sweet.

Stir in the sun-dried tomatoes, fresh coriander and paprika, fry for 1 more minute, then add the sweetcorn and season. Purée a quarter of the mixture, adding a splash of water to loosen it if the mixture is very thick.

To make the labneh, combine the cream cheese and yoghurt, season with salt to taste and spread out on a large plate. Spoon the hot sweetcorn over the labneh.

Serve with warm flatbreads or pittas.

labneh, tomato, cucumber and za'atar

Our food memories are often punctuated by 'first bites' that stay with us and we love the way, like with music, we are immediately transported back to that moment and place through food. We were visiting a bakery in Beirut and the charming baker handed me a warm pitta filled with labneh, cucumber, tomato, olives, mint and za'atar. Simple ingredients, but I was mesmerised by how the fresh mint and za'atar elevated the experience to make it complex and other-worldly. Serves 4

150g cream cheese
500g Greek yoghurt
1 cucumber, peeled in strips and cut into 5mm rounds
12 cherry tomatoes, cut into quarters
1 handful Kalamata olives
2 tablespoons mint leaves, finely shredded
juice ½ lemon
2 tablespoons za'atar, mixed with 4 tablespoons extra virgin olive oil
2–4 flatbreads or pittas, warmed

To make the labneh, combine the cream cheese and yoghurt, season with salt to taste and spread out on a large plate.

Place the cucumber, tomatoes, olives, mint, lemon juice, salt and pepper in a bowl and toss gently to mix evenly. Transfer onto the labneh, then spoon over the za'atar oil.

Serve with warm flatbreads or pittas.

labneh, courgette, tomato and mint

We learnt the technique of slow-cooking courgettes while working at the River Cafe, which transforms this crisp, subtle vegetable into something unctuous, rich and sweet. Serves 4

3-4 small to medium courgettes (450g)
5 tablespoons olive oil
3 garlic cloves, thinly sliced
300g cherry tomatoes, blitzed
2 tablespoons chopped mint
2 tablespoons chopped basil
150g cream cheese
500g strained Greek yoghurt
50g roasted, salted almonds, roughly chopped
2-4 flatbreads or pittas, warmed

Slice the courgettes very thinly with a sharp knife or by using a mandolin. Place in a colander and toss well with 1 teaspoon sea salt. Leave for 15 minutes over a bowl or sink.

Meanwhile, heat a large frying pan over a medium heat and add the oil. When hot, but not smoking, fry the garlic until golden, about 1-2 minutes, then add the tomatoes and a pinch of salt. Simmer for 5 minutes, or until the tomatoes thicken to a sauce consistency.

Squeeze any excess water out of the courgettes and add them to the pan along with 3 tablespoons of the herbs. Stir well and simmer for another 5-7 minutes, until soft.

To make the labneh, combine the cream cheese and yoghurt, season with salt to taste, and spread out on a large plate. Spoon the courgettes over the labneh and scatter over the chopped almonds and remaining tablespoon of herbs.

Serve with warm flatbreads or pittas.

labneh, mushrooms, sweet herbs and chilli butter

We use 'sweet' herbs a few times in this book. These are the softer, more fragrant, delicate herbs like basil, tarragon, dill and parsley. We all know and love them when used individually, and together they become an ethereal and delicate melange of sweetness and spice, particularly good with mushrooms or chicken. Serves 4

4 tablespoons olive oil
2 garlic cloves, thinly sliced
400g mixed mushrooms – oyster, portobello, shiitake or a mixture
    of field and wild mushrooms, cleaned and sliced
2 tablespoons each chopped dill, parsley, basil and tarragon
    + extra sprigs for garnish
150g cream cheese
500g Greek yoghurt
1 portion chilli butter (page 150)
2–4 flatbreads or pittas, warmed

Place a large pan (30cm) over a medium heat and add 3 tablespoons olive oil. When hot, but not smoking, add the garlic, and when just golden add the mushrooms and a pinch of salt and pepper. Sauté for about 5 minutes, stirring occasionally, until the mushroom liquid has almost evaporated. Transfer to a bowl and set aside. If you don't have a pan this wide, cook this in two batches. Stir in the herbs and remaining olive oil and check for seasoning.

To make the labneh, combine the cream cheese and yoghurt, season with salt to taste and spread out on a large plate.

Spoon the warm mushrooms on top, followed by the extra herbs and the chilli butter. Serve with warm flatbreads or pittas.

spiced labneh, tomatoes, mint and dukkah

Try to source sweet tomatoes in season; thankfully there seems to be more choice these days, even during the winter, with Marinda and Raf varieties. These have a crunchier texture and work well with this dish, as do unripened green tomatoes at the end of the growing season, either raw, or lightly seared in a pan with a little olive oil and garlic. We first tasted spiced labneh at a Sudanese restaurant in Portobello Road prior to opening Moro. The labneh itself was fermented and fizzy on the tongue, and when mixed with fenugreek the sensation was unique. We added green chilli and nigella seeds, and this spiced labneh continues to be a daily feature on our mezze plate. Serves 4

150g cream cheese
500g Greek yoghurt
2 green chillies, deseeded and finely chopped
1 garlic clove, crushed to a paste with salt
2 teaspoons whole fenugreek seeds, boiled for 10 minutes in plenty of water, water changed, boiled for another 10 minutes, rinsed and drained
2 teaspoons nigella seeds
300g sweet tomatoes, cut into small wedges (multi-coloured heritage tomatoes look wonderful!)
3 tablespoons mint leaves, finely sliced
3 tablespoons extra virgin olive oil
½ portion dukkah (page 54)
2–4 flatbreads or pittas, warmed

To make the labneh, combine the cream cheese, yoghurt, chilli, garlic, fenugreek and nigella seeds together then season with salt to taste. Spread out on a large plate.

Toss the tomatoes, 2 tablespoons mint and olive oil in a bowl, season, then spoon over the labneh.

Sprinkle on the dukkah and remaining mint. Serve with warm flatbreads or pittas.

labneh, carrots, caraway and pistachios

Carrots and caraway is a classic combination and a perfect partner for labneh, with pistachios for crunch and colour, and mint to lift the earthiness of the carrots. Serves 4

500g carrots, sliced on the angle, about 2cm thick
3 tablespoons olive oil
2 teaspoons whole caraway seeds
2 tablespoons finely chopped mint
½ tablespoon lemon juice
a few drops orange blossom water (optional)
150g cream cheese
500g Greek yoghurt
3 tablespoons chopped pistachios
2-4 flatbreads or pittas, warmed

Preheat the oven to 200°C/400°F/gas 6.

Toss the carrots in 2 tablespoons olive oil along with the caraway seeds, salt and pepper. Place in a roasting tray and cover with foil. Transfer to the hot oven for 15 minutes, then remove the foil and roast for another 20 minutes, until soft and slightly caramelised.

Transfer the carrots to a bowl and add the mint, lemon juice, orange blossom water (if using) and the final tablespoon of olive oil, and check for seasoning.

To make the labneh, combine the cream cheese and yoghurt, season with salt to taste and spread out on a large plate. Add the warm carrots and sprinkle with pistachios.

Serve with warm flatbreads or pittas.

marinated feta, cherry tomatoes and olives

This recipe is almost too simple to include, but it is surprising how adding thyme and fennel seeds to the feta and warming it in the oven makes the experience special. Serves 4

200g feta
3 teaspoons lemon thyme leaves
2 teaspoons fennel seeds
extra virgin olive oil
300g roast cherry tomatoes
4 garlic cloves, whole, skins on
2 tablespoons Kalamata olives
toast, to serve

Preheat the oven to 200°C/400°F/gas 6.

Sprinkle the feta with the thyme, half the fennel seeds and drizzle liberally with olive oil. Leave to marinate.

Toss the tomatoes, garlic cloves, olives and remaining fennel seeds in 2 tablespoons olive oil and season with salt and pepper. Put into a roasting tray and roast for 15-20 minutes, until the tomatoes begin to soften and caramelise.

Clear a space in the middle of the tray for the feta and bake for a further 10 minutes.

Smear the feta on toast, with the roast cherry tomatoes and olives.

whipped feta

We serve this drizzled over fried aubergines and date molasses at Morito, and it is our most popular dish. This is also delicious with roast vegetables with orzo and olives (page 250), red lentil, pepper and walnut salad with tarragon (page 98) or roast red onions and beetroot with pomegranates (page 134). So simple to make and so good. Serves 4

100g feta
4 tablespoons water
3 tablespoons extra virgin olive oil

In a food processor or hand blender, blitz the feta, water and olive oil until completely smooth. Transfer to the fridge to thicken slightly.

Pictured on page 250

fried halloumi, honey and sesame

One of the quickest recipes in the book. Salty halloumi is drizzled with sweet honey, seeds and fresh mint. Be sure to eat the halloumi immediately as it does not stay soft for long. Chopped salad (page 94) or dukkah (page 54) would work well with this. Serves 4

250g halloumi, cut into 0.5cm slices
6 tablespoons runny honey, warmed through
1 teaspoon sesame seeds, lightly toasted
½ teaspoon nigella seeds
2 tablespoons small mint leaves

Place a large non-stick frying pan over a high heat and when hot, but not smoking, add the halloumi. Fry for 30 seconds, until golden on the underside, turn over, and cook for another 30 seconds.

Transfer to a plate, drizzle over the honey, sprinkle over the sesame seeds, nigella seeds and the small leaves of mint.

HIT

INTERNATIONAL

Spania

PRODUCIDO EN ESPAÑA

easy salads

Salads are tonics, and in this increasingly health-conscious world, vegetables should form the lion's share on the plate. Variety is the key – colour, texture, flavour – to really benefit from the phytonutrient richness of plants. Eat the rainbow!

kale, preserved lemon and toasted almonds

The healthiest of salads, with a subtle Moroccan accent from the preserved lemon. Be sure to massage the kale well with the dressing as this tenderises the leaf. Serves 4

2 tablespoons lemon juice
big pinch each sea salt and sugar
1 tablespoon very finely chopped preserved lemon rind (page 303)
  + a few very thin slices for serving
5 tablespoons extra virgin olive oil
200g kale, stripped off central stalk, washed and drained well
4 tablespoons roughly chopped roasted, salted almonds

Stir the lemon juice, salt, sugar, preserved lemon and olive oil together.

Rip or chop the crinkly leaves into small pieces and place in the bowl along with the almonds and preserved lemon slices. Spoon over the dressing. Toss well, massaging the dressing into the leaves.

courgette, lemon, basil and Manchego cheese

We ate this salad in a small café in the *campo* (countryside) near Vejer de la Frontera on the west coast of Andalucia. Courgettes fresh from the *huerto* (garden) were sliced super thin, salted and left to soften. Then they were dressed with lemon, olive oil, basil and shavings of Manchego. It was a revelation! We often make this in the summer at Moro. Serves 4

500g small to medium courgettes, pale/thin-skinned if possible
1 heaped teaspoon fine sea salt
1½ tablespoons lemon juice
3 tablespoons extra virgin olive oil
2 heaped tablespoons mint, chopped
3 heaped tablespoons basil, roughly torn
50g Manchego cheese or other hard sheep's cheese, such as Pecorino, shaved with a peeler
4 tablespoons roughly chopped roasted, salted almonds

Top and tail the courgettes and slice them very thinly (1–2mm) with a sharp knife or mandolin. Place in a colander and toss well with the sea salt (massage so the salt has a chance to 'cook' each slice). Leave for 20 minutes over a bowl or sink.

Squeeze the courgettes gently to get rid of excess water, then place in a bowl. Add the lemon juice, olive oil, half the mint and basil, and toss well. Arrange on a plate. Scatter over the cheese, almonds and the rest of the herbs.

Without the cheese, this salad is also delicious as a side to cooked fish or ceviche (page 170).

cucumber, tahini sauce and chilli

A refreshing salad very compatible with fish like the sea bass with migas, lemon zest, garlic and parsley (page 203). Serves 4

1 medium cucumber, peeled and sliced into thin rounds
3 tablespoons roughly chopped dill + a few extra sprigs for serving
2 tablespoons extra virgin olive oil
1 tablespoon lemon juice
1 portion tahini sauce (see below), with 2 tablespoons yoghurt and
    1 tablespoon water added
2 teaspoons finely chopped red chilli
1 teaspoon nigella seeds

Tahini sauce
1 small garlic clove, crushed to a smooth paste with good pinch salt
3 tablespoons tahini
juice ½ lemon
5 tablespoons water
3 tablespoons olive oil

Place the cucumber and dill in a bowl, pour over the olive oil and lemon juice, season with salt and pepper and toss gently.

To make the tahini sauce, combine the garlic, tahini and lemon juice, then whisk in the water, followed by the olive oil. Check for seasoning.

Now spoon over the tahini sauce and finish with the extra dill, red chilli and nigella seeds.

autumn salad

This is delicious with the roast chicken with fennel seed, garlic and thyme marinade (page 222) and the tuna with fennel seeds, oregano and chilli (page 212). Serves 4

2 tablespoons pomegranate molasses
3 tablespoons freshly squeezed pomegranate juice
1 tablespoon good-quality red wine vinegar like cabernet sauvignon (page 303) + pinch sugar if not sweet
¼ garlic clove, crushed
5 tablespoons extra virgin olive oil
1 baby gem lettuce heart (200g), outer leaves sliced across in 2cm pieces, small leaves kept whole
2 small chicory (red or white), outer leaves sliced across in 2cm pieces, small leaves kept whole
150g grapes, cut in half
1 red apple, skin on, cored, cut into thin slices
4 fresh figs, quartered, or dried figs, finely chopped
100g pomegranate seeds
3 tablespoons shredded mint
5 tablespoons roughly chopped roasted, salted almonds

Whisk the pomegranate molasses, pomegranate juice, vinegar, garlic, salt and pepper together, then slowly drizzle in the olive oil until emulsified.

Place the leaves, grapes, apple slices, figs, pomegranate seeds and mint in a large salad bowl. Pour over the dressing and toss gently.

Scatter over the almonds and serve immediately.

red cabbage, caraway and red chilli

We were struck by the simplicity and beauty of this salad. We were in Gaziantep, southern Turkey, close to the border of Syria, in a kebab restaurant (*kebap* in Turkish) called İmam Çağdaş, which is also very famous for its baklava. Gaziantep is world-famous for its pistachio production and we import ours direct from Gaziantep. Finely shredded red cabbage, parsley, red chilli, caraway, lemon and olive oil is striking to look at, clean and fresh, and is an excellent vehicle to cut through the richness and fat of the kebab. Serves 4

2 tablespoons lemon juice
5 tablespoons extra virgin olive oil
500g red cabbage, core removed, cut into 5cm chunks, thinly shredded
3 tablespoons roughly chopped flat-leaf parsley
3 tablespoons shredded mint
1 long red chilli, deseeded and finely chopped
2 tablespoons whole caraway seeds, roughly ground

In a large bowl, whisk the lemon juice and olive oil together and season with salt and pepper.

Add the cabbage, herbs, red chilli, caraway seeds and toss well. Check for seasoning and serve.

green goddess

The inspiration for this salad comes from Alice Waters' classic cookbook *Chez Panisse Vegetables*, which lived on the bookshelf at the River Cafe. The combination of sweet herbs and anchovy transforms a simple salad into something wondrous. Serves 4

1 cos or romaine heart (200g), larger leaves chopped into 2cm pieces, smaller leaves kept whole
2 baby gem lettuce hearts (200g), outer leaves sliced across in 2cm pieces, smaller leaves kept whole
2 heads of chicory (red or white), outer leaves sliced across into 2cm pieces, smaller leaves kept whole
2 avocados, cut in half, then into thin 2mm slices
2 tablespoons each chopped chives, coriander, tarragon and basil + extra sprigs for serving
½ shallot (40g), very finely chopped
½ garlic clove, crushed with a little salt
4 good-quality Ortiz anchovy fillets in olive oil (page 304), finely chopped (optional, omit for a vegan version)
1½ tablespoons good-quality aged white wine or moscatel vinegar (page 303) + pinch sugar if not sweet
1 teaspoon Dijon mustard
1 tablespoon lemon juice
6 tablespoons extra virgin olive oil

Place the lettuce, chicory, avocado and the herbs in a large salad bowl.

Mix the shallot, garlic, anchovies (if using), vinegar, mustard and lemon juice together, then add the olive oil and season with salt and black pepper. Pour over the salad and toss well.

Serve with some extra herbs scattered on top. You can use any combination of salad leaves at your fingertips.

watermelon, cos and feta

A classic worth including – great as a salad on its own or a perfect partner to roast chicken. Try to source pumpkin seeds as they are similar to watermelon seeds; nutritious and add a pleasing crunch alongside the toasted bread. Watermelons in season, i.e. in the summer, do make a difference. Serves 4

½ loaf ciabatta bread (150g), torn into 2cm cubes
8 tablespoons extra virgin olive oil
600g watermelon, cut into 3cm cubes
½ cucumber, peeled and chopped
1 cos or romaine heart (350g), chopped
1 gem lettuce heart, chopped
2 tablespoons mint leaves
100g feta, crumbled
1 tablespoon sweet/aged red wine vinegar like cabernet sauvignon
   (page 303) + pinch sugar if not sweet
2 tablespoons pumpkin seeds, lightly toasted and salted

Heat the oven to 200°C/400°F/gas 6.

Place the bread in a large roasting tin, toss with 2 tablespoons olive oil and season with salt. Bake in the oven for 10–15 minutes, until golden and crisp but not too hard. Remove from the heat and leave to cool.

Put the toasted bread, watermelon, cucumber, lettuce, mint and feta into a large salad bowl.

Whisk the vinegar, remaining olive oil, salt and pepper together and pour over the salad. Toss carefully and serve with the pumpkin seeds sprinkled on top.

chopped salad

This goes with just about everything. You can add an avocado for variety and creaminess. This fresh salad is great with *ful medames* (page 142), tuna with fennel seeds, oregano and chilli (page 212), fried monkfish with lemon, garlic, coriander and dill (page 208), roast chicken with fenugreek and coriander marinade (page 222) or Maghrebi slow-roast shoulder of lamb (page 245). Serves 4

½ small red onion, finely diced
½ medium cucumber, peeled and finely diced (200g)
10 cherry tomatoes, halved and finely diced
1 tablespoon each roughly chopped mint, flat-leaf parsley and coriander
½ garlic clove, crushed to a paste with a little salt
squeeze lemon juice
½ tablespoon red wine vinegar + pinch sugar if not sweet
3 tablespoons extra virgin olive oil

Put all the ingredients into a bowl. Toss well and season with salt and pepper.

Serve chilled for a fresher taste.

Pictured on page 143

beetroot, apple and mint

The health benefits of this salad are obvious, and it is satisfying to make something so healthy that is equally delicious and easy to assemble.
Serves 4

2½ tablespoons good-quality sweet/aged red wine vinegar like cabernet sauvignon (page 303) or cider vinegar + pinch sugar if not sweet
4 tablespoons extra virgin olive oil
450g raw beetroot, peeled and coarsely grated
2 Granny Smith apples, skin on, cored and sliced into thin matchsticks
5 tablespoons thinly shredded mint
100g toasted walnuts, sliced

Whisk the vinegar, olive oil, salt and black pepper together. Set aside.

Combine the beetroot, apple, half the mint and half the walnuts in a large bowl, pour over the dressing and toss gently together. Check for seasoning.

Serve with the rest of the mint and walnuts scattered on top. This is also delicious with labneh (page 37).

Pictured on pages 96-7

red lentil, pepper and walnut salad with tarragon

This is an adaptation of a recipe in *A Taste of Sun and Fire: Gaziantep Cookery,* edited by our friend Aylin Öney Tan. Swap out the butter for olive oil to make this vegan. The bulgur salad can be served warm or at room temperature. Delicious with Greek yoghurt on the side or whipped feta (page 73). Serves 4

200g red lentils, rinsed well and drained
1 litre water
100g butter
2 banana shallots (120g), finely chopped
2 garlic cloves, finely chopped
1 heaped teaspoon baharat
2 red romero peppers (200g), grilled until soft, peeled and deseeded
6 sun-dried tomatoes (we use the dehydrated ones and rehydrate them
   in a bowl of just-boiled water until soft)
150g medium bulgur, covered with boiling water and left for 10 minutes
2 teaspoons Aleppo chilli flakes (page 304)
3 tablespoons pomegranate molasses
100g toasted walnuts, roughly chopped
6 tablespoons chopped tarragon + extra leaves to serve
4 tablespoons roughly chopped flat-leaf parsley
2 spring onions, finely chopped

To serve
inner leaves from 1–2 heads romaine or cos lettuce
3 tablespoons pomegranate seeds
2 tablespoons extra virgin olive oil with 2 tablespoons pomegranate juice
2 limes, cut into wedges

Place the lentils in a saucepan and cover them with 1 litre of cold water. Bring to a simmer over a medium heat, skimming off any scum, and cook for about 10–15 minutes or until tender. Remove from the heat, pour off any excess liquid, then transfer to a large bowl and allow to cool for 10 minutes.

Meanwhile, place a frying pan over a medium heat and add the butter. When it begins to foam, add the shallots, garlic and baharat and fry for 8–10 minutes, until soft and sweet.

Blitz the peppers, sun-dried tomatoes and the shallot mixture together in a food processor. Add this to the lentils and season well with salt and pepper. Now fluff up the bulgur so there are no lumps and stir this in, along with the chilli flakes, pomegranate molasses, walnuts, herbs and spring onions. Check for seasoning.

Serve on crisp young lettuce leaves scattered with a few pomegranate seeds and extra tarragon, drizzled with a little of the oil and the pomegranate dressing, with lime wedges to squeeze over.

easy veg

The future is plant food. We love vegetables and we love Spanish cuisine, but it is limited on the greens front. One of the reasons we chose the Moorish path was the plethora of vegetarian recipes from North Africa, the Middle East and the Eastern Mediterranean at our fingertips, and the balance it would bring to our menu.

artichoke salsa with olives, capers and sun-dried tomatoes

Delicious with labneh (page 37), kale purée with polenta (page 128), lentils, peas, asparagus and broad beans (page 158), fish or pork fillet with roast peppers (page 228). Serves 4

4 large globe artichokes, or 300g artichoke hearts in olive oil, drained
5 tablespoons Kalamata olives (or any good-quality olives with the stones in), pitted and chopped
1 tablespoon capers, soaked in 3 changes of water, squeezed dry and chopped
5 sun-dried tomatoes, finely chopped (we use the dehydrated ones and rehydrate them in a bowl of just-boiled water until soft)
2 teaspoons fresh thyme leaves
1 tablespoon lemon juice
2 tablespoons finely chopped flat-leaf parsley
4 tablespoons extra virgin olive oil

To cook the artichokes, follow the instructions on page 105. Drain and cool upside down in a colander. When cool enough to handle, turn the artichokes the right way up and remove all the leaves, taking care not to rip off away the heart from the base of the leaves. Remove the hairy choke from the centre with a teaspoon and discard until only the edible heart remains.

Cut each artichoke heart into quarters, then thinly slice and combine with all the other ingredients in a large bowl. Toss well and season with black pepper and a little salt if needed.

spiced potato cake

This is a great breakfast accompaniment to shakshuka (page 44) or any eggs or labneh (pages 37-71), spring greens with crispy chorizo (page 124), veal escalopes, rosemary and jamón (page 233), roast shoulder of pork marinated with orange and cumin (page 238), mussels with yoghurt, dill and crispy chickpeas (page 190) or squid kofte with *mojo verde* (page 184).
Serves 4

4 potatoes (500g), peeled
½ banana shallot (40g), finely grated
3 teaspoons roughly ground coriander seeds
3 teaspoons roughly ground cumin seeds
2 teaspoons thyme leaves
2 tablespoons olive oil
20g butter + extra knob

Grate the potatoes on a coarse grater, place in a bowl, then cover with cold water and massage a bit to wash out some of the starch. Leave for 5 minutes, drain well, squeeze out any excess water and spread out between kitchen cloths to dry.

Toss the potato with the grated shallot, spices, thyme and season with salt.

Place a large non-stick frying pan (30cm) over a medium to high heat and when hot, add the olive oil and butter. When the butter begins to foam, add the spiced raw potato to the pan and flatten to about 0.5cm, depending on the width of your pan. Fry for 5-8 minutes, or until the potatoes combine to form a cake and the underside is crisp and golden. Turn over with a spatula and cook for a further 4-6 minutes, adding a little extra butter that will run down the sides, giving extra crispiness. Once both sides are crisp and golden brown, remove from the pan and rest briefly on kitchen paper before serving.

boiled artichokes with za'atar

A simple dipping sauce for artichokes with a Lebanese twist instead of the classic vinaigrette. Also great with lentils, peas, asparagus and broad beans (page 158). Serves 4

4 large globe artichokes, stalks removed
1 tablespoon lemon juice
1 garlic clove, crushed with a little salt
1 level teaspoon caster sugar
6 teaspoons za'atar
100ml extra virgin olive oil

Cook the artichokes in boiling salted water for 20–30 minutes, or until tender (when the leaves at the base can be pulled away easily and the base is tender when you insert a sharp knife). Drain in a colander and leave the artichokes upside down to cool.

Meanwhile, whisk the lemon juice, garlic, sugar and za'atar together, then slowly drizzle in the olive oil and season with salt and pepper.

Cut the artichokes in half lengthways. Remove the hairy choke with a small knife or teaspoon (it should come out in clumps) and discard, along with some of the central lighter leaves.

Drizzle some of the za'atar dressing over the artichoke hearts and serve the rest on the side for dipping the leaves.

Pictured on pages 106-7

roasted aubergines, tomatoes and tahini

Delicious with fish or chicken or as part of a vegetable mezze. Omit the yoghurt to keep it dairy-free. Serves 4

200g ripe tomatoes, blitzed or finely chopped
½ garlic clove, crushed to a paste with salt
2 aubergines, sliced into 1cm rounds, sprinkled with fine salt
   and left in a colander for 20 minutes
olive oil for brushing
1 portion tahini sauce (page 83), with 2 tablespoons Greek yoghurt
   and 1 tablespoon water added
2 teaspoons za'atar
2 tablespoons finely shredded mint

Preheat the oven to 220°C/425°F/gas 7.

Mix the blitzed tomato with the garlic and season to taste.

Pat the aubergines dry with a cloth and brush both sides of the slices liberally with olive oil. Place in a large roasting tin (or two smaller tins) brushed with olive oil and roast for 20 minutes until golden on the underside. Turn over and add 1 teaspoon of the blended tomato mix on top of each round. Return to the oven for another 5 minutes.

Remove and serve warm or at room temperature with about 1 teaspoon tahini yoghurt, a sprinkle of za'atar and mint on each round.

roasted aubergines, pomegranates and pistachios

We had the privilege of travelling around Syria in 2009. This is one of the dishes we returned with. This is delicious with fish, like tuna with fennel seeds, oregano and chilli (page 212) or a spoonful of labneh (page 37) or tahini on the side. Serves 4

2 aubergines, diced into 1.5cm cubes, sprinkled with fine salt
  and left in a colander for 20 minutes
5 tablespoons olive oil
3 tablespoons fresh pomegranate juice
2 tablespoons pomegranate molasses
4 tablespoons pomegranate seeds
2 tablespoons finely shredded flat-leaf parsley
2 tablespoons finely shredded mint
25g pistachios, roughly chopped

Preheat the oven to 220°C/425°F/gas 7.

Pat the aubergines dry with a cloth and toss with 4 tablespoons olive oil. Place in a large roasting tray and roast for 20 minutes, tossing after 15 minutes, until golden brown and caramelised on all sides. Remove and transfer to a large plate or salad bowl.

Mix the pomegranate juice, pomegranate molasses, remaining tablespoon of olive oil, salt and pepper. Check the seasoning, then spoon over the aubergines and toss gently.

Sprinkle over the pomegranate seeds, parsley, mint and pistachios and serve.

fried courgettes with *cacık*

Cacık is the Turkish version of Greek tzatziki, with dill instead of mint. It is a cooling dip for these hot, crispy courgettes. Also delicious with fish or meat.
Serves 4

500g courgettes, cut into thin batons/thick matchsticks
1 litre sunflower oil

Batter
40g plain flour
40g cornflour
140ml cold soda or fizzy water
pinch baking powder
pinch salt
1 litre sunflower oil, for frying

Cacık
1 cucumber (400g), peeled in strips, coarsely grated
200g Greek yoghurt
1 garlic clove, crushed with salt
1 tablespoon extra virgin olive oil
3 tablespoons chopped dill + a few extra sprigs
1 teaspoon chopped red chilli

First place the courgettes in a colander, sprinkle with fine sea salt, and leave for 20 minutes.

Make the batter by mixing together all the ingredients (except the oil) with your fingers or a balloon whisk. Rest for 15 minutes.

For the *cacık*, mix all the ingredients together (except the chilli and extra dill sprigs) and check for seasoning.

When you are ready to fry the courgettes, heat the sunflower oil in a large high-sided saucepan until very hot, but not smoking, making sure the oil does not come more than halfway up the pan. Dry the courgettes well with a cloth, then dip them lightly into the batter, allowing any excess to drip off, and fry a few at a time in the oil until golden. Drain on kitchen paper to absorb excess oil and sprinkle lightly with salt.

Serve with the *cacık*, with the extra dill sprigs and chopped red chilli scattered on top.

gem lettuce, peas and pancetta

We adore the sweetness and soft texture of cooked lettuce. This dish is just wonderful on its own or as a side with fish or chicken - scallops with Albariño wine (page 198), turbot with anchovy, rosemary and paprika butter (page 204), sea bass with migas (page 203), roast chicken with fennel seed, garlic and thyme marinade (page 222), veal escalopes (page 233) - or lamb chops and hot mint sauce (page 241). Serves 4

2 tablespoons olive oil
150g smoked pancetta, lardons or bacon, cut into thick matchsticks
    or 1cm cubes
1 banana shallot (60g), finely chopped
2 garlic cloves, sliced
1 tablespoon thyme leaves
40g butter
4 gem lettuce hearts, stalks trimmed, cut in half lengthways
70ml medium white wine or water
200g petit pois or peas, fresh or frozen
4 tablespoons crème fraîche or cream
2 tablespoons finely chopped mint

Place a wide frying pan over a medium to high heat and add the olive oil and pancetta. Fry, stirring occasionally, until starting to crisp, about 5 minutes. Add the shallot, garlic and thyme and fry for another 5 minutes, stirring regularly, until caramelised. Transfer the mixture to a bowl and set aside.

Add the butter to the pan and when it starts to foam, add the gem lettuces, cut side down. Fry for 6-7 minutes then turn and fry for another 2 minutes until golden brown on both sides. Season with salt and pepper. Add a splash of wine or water and the peas, pop the lid on and simmer for 30 seconds. Add the crème fraîche and pancetta mixture then continue to cook for a couple more minutes.

Serve with the mint on top.

roast squash, sweet vinegar, garlic and rosemary

The sweetness of the squash contrasts beautifully with the vinegar. Delicious with labneh (page 37), fish, chicken or lamb, like the Maghrebi slow-roast shoulder of lamb (page 245) or tomato bulgur with lamb and cinnamon yoghurt (page 271). Serves 4

1 large butternut squash or sweet potatoes, approx. 800g, peeled, deseeded and cut into 3cm chunks
5 tablespoons olive oil
1 teaspoon ground cinnamon
2 garlic cloves, thinly sliced
3 tablespoons finely chopped rosemary
3 tablespoons aged, good-quality red wine vinegar like cabernet sauvignon, or sherry vinegar (page 303) + pinch sugar if not sweet
1–2 teaspoons finely chopped red chilli (to taste)

Preheat the oven to 200°C/400°F/gas 6.

Toss the squash with 2 tablespoons olive oil, the cinnamon, salt and pepper. Lay on a large roasting tray and roast in the oven for 20 minutes, until soft and caramelised. Check for seasoning.

Meanwhile, heat the remaining olive oil over a low to medium heat. Add the garlic and rosemary and fry gently for 2–3 minutes until the garlic is golden, then add the vinegar, taking care it doesn't spit too much, and simmer for 30 seconds (see photo on page 120). Spoon the vinegar mixture over the squash and serve with the chilli on top.

asparagus, orange butter sauce and toasted hazelnuts

We all look forward to the British asparagus season that starts in April, weather depending. There are so many ways to serve asparagus; this is one of our favourites, though other variations include labneh, chilli butter, and dukkah (page 54), anchovy, rosemary and paprika butter (page 204), or scallops and lemon thyme (page 201). Serves 4

1 heaped teaspoon orange zest
100ml orange juice
2 tablespoons lemon juice
2 bay leaves
sprig of thyme
150g unsalted butter, in cubes
28–32 green asparagus spears (depending on thickness),
   tough woody ends snapped off
4 tablespoons roughly chopped, lightly toasted blanched hazelnuts

Place the orange zest, orange and lemon juice, bay leaves and thyme in a saucepan and simmer over a low heat for 2 minutes. Remove the herbs and start to whisk in the butter, a couple of cubes at a time, until it is all incorporated and the sauce has emulsified. Season with salt to taste. Keep warm.

Meanwhile bring a large pot of lightly salted water to the boil over a high heat and blanch the asparagus spears for 3–5 minutes, depending on their thickness, or until tender. Drain well.

Serve immediately, with the warm orange butter sauce over the asparagus, and the toasted hazelnuts scattered on top.

spring greens with crispy chorizo

Shredding the greens thinly is an important part of this dish, creating texture. It is similar to the shredded greens for Caldo Verde, the delicious Portuguese potato, chorizo and greens soup that we learnt to make at the Eagle Pub and is still one of our favourites. Fennel seeds are recommended to add another dimension, though not essential. Serves 4

400-500g (2-4 heads) spring greens, washed
2 tablespoons olive oil
100g cooking chorizo (page 304), cut into quarters lengthways, then into 1cm cubes
2 garlic cloves, thinly sliced
2 heaped teaspoons fennel seeds (optional)

Cut off the base of the spring greens and 2cm of hard stalk closest to the base and discard. Keeping the leaves together, roll them into a tight cylinder. Using a very sharp knife, slice the leaves in half lengthways then shred across very thinly (no more than 0.5cm wide).

In a large, wide frying pan or saucepan (30cm), heat the oil over a medium heat. When hot, add the chorizo, garlic and fennel seeds (if using) and fry for 4-5 minutes, stirring occasionally, until the chorizo is a little crispy and caramelised. Take care that the garlic does not get too dark. Remove half the chorizo with a slotted spoon, set aside and keep warm.

Add the greens to the pan, season with salt and pepper and stir well for 3-4 minutes, or until the greens are soft and tender. Check for seasoning and serve immediately with the rest of the chorizo on top.

seared mushrooms with Manchego

Last October we managed to escape to the hills of the Sierra Norte, north of Seville, and caught the end of the wild mushroom season. We devoured a plate of Caesar's mushrooms, *Amanita caesarea,* which were simply seared and served with shavings of Manchego and a wedge of orange. Orange instead of lemon was genius, and so obvious, but the idea had never occurred to us. This dish can be made with a variety of mushrooms – wild mushrooms during the autumn or oyster mushrooms. Serves 4

400g oyster mushrooms (thick stalks trimmed) or a mix of oyster and wild, cleaned and sliced if large
1 garlic clove, very finely chopped
3 teaspoons lemon thyme leaves
4 tablespoons extra virgin olive oil + extra for drizzling
30g Manchego or other hard sheep's cheese, such as Pecorino, shaved with a peeler
1 orange, cut into wedges

Place the mushrooms in a bowl and toss with salt, pepper, garlic, half the thyme and the olive oil. Heat a large, wide frying pan over a high heat. When the pan is very hot, add a third to half of the mushrooms (depending on the size of your pan) in a single layer and press down with a spatula or spoon. Cook for a minute and a half then turn and cook for another 30 seconds on the second side, until golden brown on both sides. Transfer them to a bowl and repeat with the rest of the mushrooms, remembering not to overcrowd the pan.

Lay the mushrooms on a large plate, drizzle over a little extra olive oil, the remaining thyme and the Manchego shavings. Check for seasoning and serve with orange wedges to squeeze over.

kale purée with polenta

Every mouthful is moreish and wholesome. This is so good as an accompaniment to roast chicken or fish, with perhaps artichoke salsa with olives, capers and sun-dried tomatoes (page 102), or simply with some Manchego or other hard sheep's cheese grated on top. Serves 4

4 tablespoons olive oil
5 garlic cloves, finely chopped
200g kale, stripped off the central stalk, washed, drained
   and roughly chopped
750ml water
5 rounded tablespoons instant polenta
1 teaspoon freshly grated nutmeg
50g butter

Place a large saucepan over a medium to high heat and add the olive oil. When hot, but not smoking, add the garlic and fry until golden/pale brown. Add the kale and a pinch of salt and stir for a few seconds until the kale begins to wilt. Add the water and bring to a gentle simmer for 3–5 minutes or until the kale is just tender. Remove from the heat and purée the kale while still in the pan with a hand blender (or in a food processor) until just smooth.

Add the polenta and return to the heat for 5 minutes, stirring occasionally. The purée should thicken to the consistency of wet mashed potato. Add the nutmeg, half the butter and some black pepper, check for salt and serve immediately, with the rest of the butter on top.

spinach, pine nuts and sultanas

For a more substantial meal, serve on toast with a dollop of soft goat's cheese on top to melt into the warm, sweet spinach. This recipe is endlessly compatible and goes with most of the recipes in the fish chapter, as well as the brown rice and potato pilaf (page 149) or the leek, pepper and walnut bulgur pilaf (page 153). It is also delicious with duck breasts with walnut and pomegranate sauce (page 226), veal escalopes, rosemary and jamón (page 233), roast shoulder of pork marinated with orange and cumin (page 238) and more! Serves 4

1kg spinach, washed and drained
4 tablespoons olive oil
2 banana shallots (120g), very finely chopped
1 garlic clove, finely chopped
½ teaspoon dried oregano or 1 teaspoon finely chopped fresh oregano
5 tablespoons pine nuts, lightly toasted
5 tablespoons sultanas
100–150g soft goat's cheese (optional)
toast (optional)

Wilt the washed spinach in a wide dry pan (30cm) in two to three batches over a medium heat. When soft, transfer to a colander to drain and cool. Squeeze out any excess water and roughly chop.

Rinse the pan quickly then return to the heat and add the olive oil. Once hot, add the shallots, garlic, oregano and a pinch of salt. Fry for 8–10 minutes, stirring occasionally, until soft and caramelised. Add the pine nuts and sultanas, then fry for a minute. Add the spinach, stir to warm through.

Check for seasoning and serve, either as it is, or on toast with some goat's cheese.

roast red onions and beetroot with pomegranates

A perfect accompaniment to fish or meat, with thyme dressing (page 201) or with labneh (page 37), whipped feta (page 73) or soft goat's cheese.
Serves 4

500g bunched beetroots, peeled
500g red onions, peeled
1 tablespoon finely chopped rosemary or thyme
3 tablespoons olive oil
4 tablespoons pomegranate molasses
½ tablespoon red wine vinegar, like cabernet sauvignon (page 303)
3 tablespoons pomegranate seeds
1 tablespoon shredded mint

Preheat the oven to 200°C/400°F/gas 6.

Cut the beetroots and onions into thin wedges, 2cm wide at their thickest point. Place in a large roasting tray, toss with the the rosemary or thyme, olive oil, pomegranate molasses, vinegar and a pinch of salt, and cover with foil. Roast for 30 minutes, then remove the foil, toss again and continue to roast for 30-40 minutes until soft, tender and caramelised.

Serve with the pomegranate seeds and mint sprinkled on top.

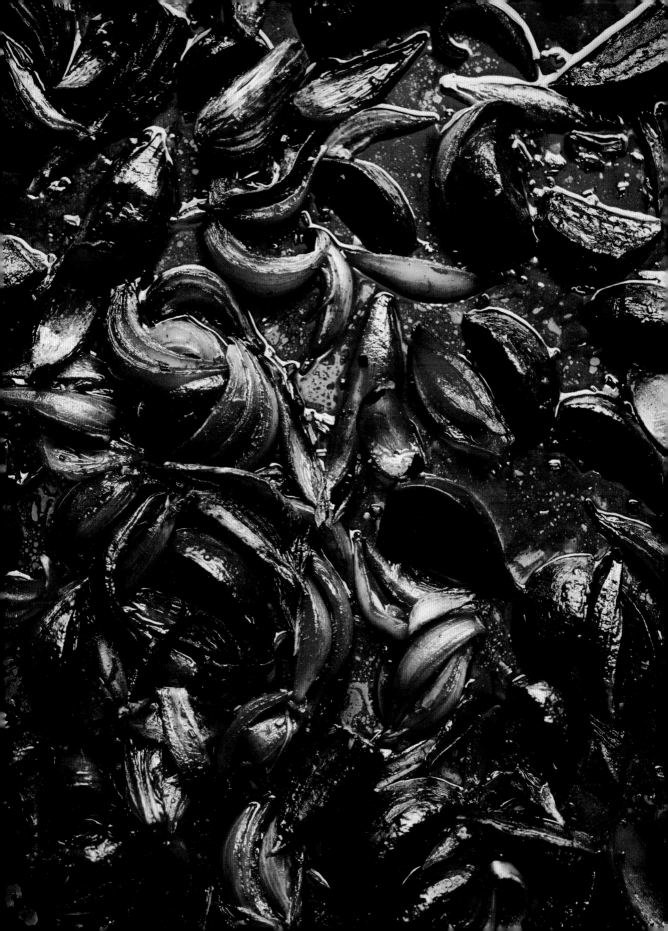

fried potatoes with za'atar, peppers and feta

We love the texture of the creamy, soft and salty feta gently melting into the potatoes as they are tossed together. You can see how it is a versatile accompaniment to fish and meat dishes. Also delicious with a simple tomato and basil salad. Serves 4

1kg roasting potatoes, e.g. Maris Piper, peeled and
    cut into quarters or sixths, depending on size
2 tablespoons olive oil
50g butter
3 garlic cloves, finely chopped
1 heaped tablespoon za'atar
4 spring onions (white and green parts), thinly sliced
2 tablespoons chopped coriander
150g piquillo peppers (or any other roast peppers from a jar),
    drained and sliced into thin strips
75g feta, crumbled

Boil the potatoes in salted water for 7–10 minutes, until just tender, then drain in a colander and spread out to dry and cool. Rough up the edges of the potatoes with a fork.

Put the olive oil and butter into a large frying pan (30cm) over a medium heat, and when the butter starts to foam, add the garlic and fry gently for a minute until very lightly golden. Add the potatoes to the pan and stir well. Season with a little more salt and pepper then fry gently for 10–15 minutes, turning occasionally and taking care the garlic doesn't burn, until golden and crisp on all sides.

Remove the pan from the heat and transfer the potatoes to a dish. Sprinkle over the za'atar, spring onions, coriander and peppers, and toss gently.

Finally crumble over the feta, toss once more, check for seasoning and serve.

peas with jamón and mint

Recommended with veal escalopes, rosemary and jamón (page 233), scallops with Albariño wine (page 198), sea bass with migas, lemon zest, garlic and parsley (page 203) and pork fillet with roast peppers (page 228). Serves 4

3 tablespoons olive oil
2 garlic cloves, thinly sliced
1 teaspoon fennel seeds or whole anise
2 bay leaves
30g jamón ibérico or jamón serrano, cut into thin matchsticks
400g frozen petit pois or garden peas
4 tablespoons shredded mint

Heat the olive oil in a large pan until hot, but not smoking, then add the garlic, fennel seeds, bay leaves and jamón. Fry over a medium heat for 3-4 minutes, until the garlic is golden brown and the jamón is crispy.

Add the peas and cook for 3-4 minutes, until tender. Season to taste with salt and pepper and serve with the shredded mint on top.

MATA-HARI

MATA-HARI

MATA-HARI

MATA-HARI

MATA-HARI

MATA-HARI

MATA-HARI

MA

MATA-HARI

PRODUCIDO EN ESPAÑA
R. E. Nº 1.917
ALCIRA-VALENCIA

Spania

easy rice, grains and pulses

Rice, grains and pulses are a daily staple of Spanish and Middle Eastern cuisine. Their soft, unctuous texture and delicately spiced earthy flavours are deeply satisfying and nutritious. Whenever we travel we always seek out rice dishes or a plate of chickpeas or lentils as they are often the best thing on the menu.

ful medames

Ful is the Egyptian breakfast staple, traditionally made with whole dried broad beans, or *ful*. This makes a fresh, simple and nutritious lunch, served with flatbread to scoop it up. For an even more sustainable plate, add hard-boiled eggs and olives. Excellent with chopped salad (page 94), tahini sauce (page 83) and flatbread (page 144). Serves 4

Ful
4 tablespoons olive oil + extra for drizzling
1 leek, excess green removed, washed and finely chopped
2 garlic cloves, sliced
1 tablespoon ground cumin seeds
1 teaspoon ground coriander seeds
15 (150g) cherry tomatoes, diced
2 x 400g tins cooked *ful medames*, mixed beans or borlotti beans

To serve
chopped salad (page 94)
tahini sauce (page 83)
flatbreads or pittas, warmed
2 hard-boiled organic or free-range eggs, cut into in quarters (optional)
handful of olives
lemon wedges

Place a medium saucepan over a medium heat and add the olive oil, leek, garlic, spices and a pinch of salt. Cook for 10 minutes, stirring occasionally, until soft and a little caramelised.

Add the tomatoes, season and cook for 3 more minutes, add the beans and their liquid then gently bring to the boil, stirring slowly. Simmer for 1-2 minutes, then take off the heat. Purée half the beans with a hand blender or potato masher. Top up cautiously with boiling water so the beans are coated in the velvety sauce and check for seasoning.

To serve, spoon the warm ful onto four plates, scatter over the chopped salad, and drizzle with the tahini sauce and a little extra olive oil. Serve with warm flatbreads or pittas, and with hard-boiled eggs, olives and lemon wedges on the side.

easy flatbread

This is a quick flatbread recipe, if you want to have a go. Dipping a flatbread in the za'atar oil is a traditional way to enjoy it. Flatbreads with chopped salad (page 94) and *ful medames* (page 142) would make a perfect trio. We source excellent sustainable bread flour from Wildfarmed. See wildfarmed.co.uk to read about their mission. Makes 8-10

400ml tepid water
500g organic strong white bread flour + extra for rolling
1 teaspoon dried yeast
1 teaspoon fine sea salt
2 tablespoons za'atar mixed with 4 tablespoons extra virgin olive oil

Put all the ingredients except the za'atar and olive oil into a large bowl or a food processor with a dough hook attachment. Combine well and knead for 5 minutes if using a food processor, and a few minutes more if by hand, until the dough feels smooth and elastic. Rest the dough for 5 minutes, then knead for another 3 minutes. Rest, covered, for about 30 minutes.

Sprinkle a clean surface with flour. Knead the dough in the bowl briefly one more time, then pinch off pieces of dough a little larger than a golf ball. Sprinkle more flour on top, flatten them slightly and roll each one into a thin disc (around 3mm) with a rolling pin.

Place a large frying pan over a medium heat and, when hot, add the flatbread. Cook on both sides until lightly coloured. Serve with the za'atar oil.

Pictured on pages 146-7

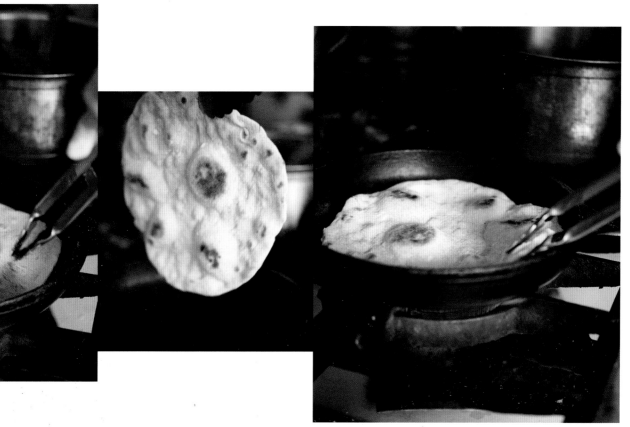

brown rice and potato pilaf

The double carbs are the key to the magic of this pilaf. The two basic ingredients combine to create an opulent and luxurious texture. Perfect with labneh, mushrooms, sweet herbs and chilli butter (page 67), spinach, pine nuts and sultanas (page 133), lamb chops (page 240), duck breasts with walnut and pomegranate sauce (page 226), roast chicken with fenugreek and coriander marinade (page 222). Serves 4

75g butter
1½ teaspoons ground cinnamon
1½ teaspoons ground allspice or baharat
2 leeks (white parts only) thinly sliced
500g potatoes, peeled, cut into 1.5cm cubes and tossed with 1 teaspoon salt
250g brown rice
700ml hot vegetable stock (2 tablespoons Marigold vegetable powder mixed with boiling water)
4 tablespoons crispy fried onions
150g Greek yoghurt, mixed with 1 garlic clove, crushed with a little salt

In a medium heavy-based saucepan, heat the butter over a medium heat. When it foams, add the cinnamon and allspice, fry for 30 seconds, then add the leeks and a pinch of salt and black pepper. Fry for 12-15 minutes, stirring occasionally, until the leeks are soft and sweet.

Add the potatoes and rice, stir well, then pour over the hot stock. Cover with a circle of baking paper and a lid and simmer gently for 30-40 minutes, or until the potatoes and rice are cooked. Remove from the heat, check for seasoning and let it rest for 5 minutes, then serve with the crispy onions on top and the yoghurt on the side.

red lentil soup with yoghurt and mint

Our Turkish chef, Turguy, first made us this simple yet deeply satisfying soup. The dried mint gives it a special aroma with added complexity from the chilli butter. Turguy's family hosted us once in Gaziantep. The table was groaning with an incredible feast, as is the way with Turkish hospitality. They couldn't speak English, we couldn't speak Turkish, but it didn't matter one bit. Serves 4

2 banana shallots (120g), each cut into 3
1 stick of celery, cut into 3
1 carrot, cut into 3
3 garlic cloves
4 tablespoons olive oil
2 heaped teaspoons ground cumin seeds
2 heaped teaspoons ground coriander seeds
½ teaspoon turmeric
2 teaspoons dried mint or 1 tablespoon chopped mint
200g tomatoes and 1 x 400g tin tomatoes, blitzed
1.2 litres vegetable stock
200g dried red lentils, rinsed well and drained
squeeze lemon juice
4 tablespoons Greek yoghurt
lemon wedges, to serve

Chilli butter
50g unsalted butter
1 heaped teaspoon Aleppo chilli flakes (page 304)

To make the chilli butter, melt the butter in a small saucepan over a low heat until it separates and the milky white bits of whey start to caramelise and smell sweet. Take off the heat and stir in the chilli flakes. Set aside.

Finely chop or blitz the shallots, celery, carrot and garlic in a food processor. Place a wide saucepan over a medium heat, and when hot, add the olive oil, blitzed vegetables, spices and mint. Season with salt and pepper and cook, stirring occasionally, for 10 minutes. Add the fresh and tinned tomatoes and simmer for another 5 minutes, until the tomatoes have broken down into a sauce. Add the stock and lentils and bring to a simmer. Cook for 15–20 minutes, or until the lentils have broken down into the stock.

Blitz a third of the soup for 5 seconds with a hand blender to bring everything together, but still with a little bit of texture, then add the lemon juice and check for seasoning. Serve with spoonfuls of yoghurt on top, and with the chilli butter and lemon wedges on the side.

leek, pepper and walnut bulgur pilaf

This is excellent with labneh, sun-dried tomato, coriander and fennel seeds (page 57), and/or red cabbage, caraway and red chilli (page 88) or chopped salad (page 94). Serves 4

100g butter
2 teaspoons ground cinnamon
1 teaspoon ground allspice or baharat
1 teaspoon smoked paprika
pinch chilli flakes
2 large leeks (white parts only), sliced into 1cm pieces
2 garlic cloves, finely chopped
2 tablespoons thyme leaves
2 red romero peppers or bell peppers, cut in half,
    deseeded and roughly chopped
200g cherry tomatoes, blitzed
250g medium or coarse bulgur, rinsed and drained
500ml hot flavoursome vegetable stock (2 tablespoons Marigold
    vegetable powder mixed with boiling water)
4 tablespoons walnuts, roughly chopped
3 tablespoons each roughly chopped dill and flat-leaf parsley
chilli butter to serve (optional, page 150)
150g Greek yoghurt, mixed with 1 garlic clove, crushed with a little salt

In a medium (20cm) heavy-based saucepan, heat the butter over a medium heat. When it foams, add the cinnamon, allspice, paprika and chilli flakes and fry for 30 seconds, then add the leeks, garlic, thyme, red peppers and a pinch of salt. Stir well and continue to fry for 15–20 minutes, stirring occasionally, until the leeks and peppers are soft and sweet.

Add the tomatoes, cook for another 5 minutes, then stir in the bulgur and the hot stock. Check for seasoning, cover with a circle of baking paper and a lid, and simmer gently for 15–20 minutes, or until the bulgur has absorbed the stock and is cooked.

Remove from the heat and let it rest for 5 minutes. Just before serving, stir in the walnuts, and serve with the herbs and chilli butter (if using) on top and the yoghurt on the side.

oyster mushroom broth with barley and sweet herbs

In this Georgian recipe, the mushrooms work beautifully with the tomatoes, pearl barley and sweet herbs to create a cleansing, nutritious and satisfying broth. Serves 4

125g pearl barley
1 litre water
5 tablespoons olive oil + extra to drizzle
1 leek (white part only), finely chopped
4 spring onions (white and green parts), finely chopped
3 garlic cloves, finely chopped
3 teaspoons ground coriander seeds
400g oyster mushrooms, tough stalks removed, roughly chopped
30g dried porcini, steeped in 50ml boiling water, drained and chopped (reserve the liquid)
400g ripe tomatoes, blitzed or finely chopped
200g tinned tomatoes, blitzed or finely chopped
1 teaspoon smoked paprika
700ml hot flavoursome vegetable stock (2 tablespoons Marigold vegetable powder mixed with boiling water)
3 tablespoons each roughly chopped tarragon, dill, basil and flat-leaf parsley
4 tablespoons Greek yoghurt

Simmer the barley in 1 litre of water, lid on, for about 40–45 minutes, until tender, then drain.

Heat the olive oil in a large, high-sided frying pan (30cm) over a medium heat and fry the leek, spring onions, garlic and ground coriander seeds, with a pinch of salt and pepper, for 8–10 minutes, stirring occasionally. Add the oyster and porcini mushrooms, season, and continue to cook for 15 minutes, stirring occasionally until lightly caramelised.

Add the fresh and tinned tomatoes and the paprika and simmer for 15 more minutes, until the tomatoes have broken down into a sauce, then pour in the stock and reserved porcini soaking liquid. Add the barley and two-thirds of the herbs. Bring to a gentle simmer and season once more.

Serve with yoghurt and the rest of the herbs on top, and an extra drizzle of olive oil.

lentils, peas, asparagus and broad beans

The lentils seem to enhance the flavour and texture of the spring vegetables in this recipe. We recommend this with the turbot with anchovy, rosemary and paprika butter (page 204), sea bass with migas, lemon zest, garlic and parsley (page 203), mackerel with tomato, olive and sherry vinaigrette (page 210), roast chicken (page 222), roast shoulder of pork marinated with orange and cumin (page 238) or lamb chops with hot mint sauce (page 240) or a soft goat's cheese. Serves 4

170g small green or brown lentils, rinsed and drained
½ stick celery
2 garlic cloves, halved
1 tablespoon finely chopped rosemary
3 sage leaves (optional)
4 tablespoons extra virgin olive oil
juice ½ lemon
150g podded broad beans
200g petits pois or peas (frozen are fine)
8 green asparagus spears, woody ends snapped off, cut into 2cm lengths
2 tablespoons each roughly chopped basil, tarragon, mint and dill
　+ extra sprigs for garnish

Place the lentils, celery, garlic, rosemary and sage (if using) in a saucepan, cover with water and bring to a gentle simmer for 15-20 minutes, until the lentils are tender but have not lost their shape. Pour off the cooking liquid until just under the level of the lentils and remove the aromatics. Add the olive oil and lemon juice, and season well with salt and pepper.

Meanwhile, bring a large pot of unsalted water to a rolling boil. First blanch the broad beans for a couple of minutes until tender, then remove with a slotted spoon and cool in a colander under running water. If the broad beans are large and the pale outer skins are tough, remove the outer skins. Add salt to the boiling water and blanch the peas and asparagus separately, cool as before, then set aside.

To finish, add the blanched vegetables and chopped herbs to the lentils and serve with the extra herb sprigs on top.

erişte with leeks, yoghurt and walnuts

Erişte is a hand-rolled Turkish pasta traditionally made for the winter. We ate this classic *erişte* dish with walnuts and yoghurt when travelling around Anatolia and added caramelised leeks for sweetness and chilli for a little kick. Serves 4

4 medium leeks, washed, outer leaves and dark green parts removed
75g butter
1 level teaspoon ground baharat or allspice
1 level teaspoon dried mint
200g small dried pasta, such as *erişte*, macaroni, trofie or small
  conchiglie (shells)
10 tablespoons Greek yoghurt
75g walnuts, lightly toasted and roughly chopped
1 portion chilli butter (page 150) or 2 teaspoons finely chopped red chilli

Cut the leeks into quarters lengthways and then across into 2cm pieces.

Melt the butter in a large, wide frying pan or saucepan over a low to medium heat until the butter separates and the whey turns golden and smells like caramel. Add the leeks, baharat, dried mint and a good pinch of salt and cook for 8–10 minutes, stirring occasionally, until soft and sweet. Set aside.

Boil the pasta in a large pot of salted water according to the packet instructions. Reserve a large mug of pasta water before draining and immediately returning the pasta to the pan with the leeks. Add the yoghurt, half the walnuts and a splash of the reserved pasta water. Toss carefully and if the sauce is a little thick, add another splash of pasta water to loosen. Check for seasoning.

Serve immediately, with the chilli butter and the rest of the walnuts scattered on top.

spinach and chickpeas

Try this with labneh, sun-dried tomato, coriander and fennel seeds (page 57), shakshuka (page 44), artichoke salsa with olives, capers and sun-dried tomatoes (page 102), squid kofte with *mojo verde* (page 184), tuna with fennel seeds, oregano and chilli (page 212), fried monkfish with lemon, garlic, coriander and dill (page 208), roast chicken with fenugreek and coriander marinade (page 222) and yoghurt or roast shoulder of pork marinated with orange and cumin (page 238). Serves 4

1kg spinach, washed and drained
7 tablespoons olive oil
2 leeks, trimmed and finely chopped
3 garlic cloves, thinly sliced
2 teaspoons ground cumin seeds
½ teaspoon dried oregano
200g cherry tomatoes, finely chopped or blitzed
2 x 400g tinned cooked chickpeas, drained
pinch saffron, steeped in 4 tablespoons boiling water (optional)
550ml water

To serve (optional)
migas (fried bread, page 203), without the garlic and parlsey
zest ½ lemon
150g Greek yoghurt

Wilt the washed spinach in a wide dry pan (30cm) in two to three batches over a medium heat. Drain in a colander and cool, then squeeze lightly and roughly chop.

Rinse the pan and return it to the heat, and add 5 tablespoons olive oil. Once hot, add the leeks, garlic, cumin, oregano and season, then cook for 10-15 minutes, stirring occasionally, until the leeks are soft and sweet. Stir in the tomatoes, chickpeas, saffron water (if using) and 300ml water. Simmer gently for 15 minutes.

With a potato masher, crush a quarter of the chickpeas. Add the spinach, remaining olive oil and a further 250ml water. Simmer for 5 minutes, check for seasoning and serve with the migas and lemon zest on top, and the yoghurt on the side.

lentils and chorizo

Whenever we are in Spain, we always seek out the *guisos*, *pucheros*, *potajes* or *cocidos* that appear on many *menus del dia* 'for the workers' lunch market. These are simple plates of slow-cooked beans or pulses flavoured with a little bit of salted pork, jamón or chorizo, a few vegetables and sometimes saffron, cooked in a pressure cooker so the pulses become incredibly soft. This is a really satisfying dish on its own, but it is also delicious with roast chicken with fennel seed, garlic and thyme marinade (page 222) or served over some nutty brown rice. Serves 4

2 tablespoons olive oil + extra to drizzle
150g cooking chorizo, cut into quarters lengthways, then into 1cm pieces
2 garlic cloves, thinly sliced
2 carrots (150g), peeled and cut into 1cm pieces
2 banana shallots (120g), cut into 1cm pieces
2 sticks of celery (150g), cut into 1cm pieces
2 bay leaves
2 tablespoons finely chopped rosemary
2 potatoes (250g), peeled and cut into 1cm pieces
250g small brown or green lentils, e.g. Puy, rinsed and drained
1.3 litres water
4 tablespoons roughly chopped parsley

Place a large (25cm) saucepan over a medium heat and add the olive oil. When hot, add the chorizo and fry for 5–8 minutes, until caramelised and lightly crisp. Remove half the chorizo, set aside and keep warm.

Add the garlic, carrots, shallots, celery, bay leaves and rosemary, season with salt and pepper, then fry for 10 minutes until soft and beginning to caramelise, stirring occasionally.

Add the potatoes and lentils and just cover with 1.3 litres water. Simmer for 25 minutes, or until the lentils are soft but still have their shape. Check the seasoning.

Serve with the parsley and the rest of the chorizo on top, plus an extra drizzle of olive oil.

easy fish

Eating seafood is a treat and it must be cooked and enjoyed with respect as oceans continue to be plundered by trawlers. Always choose seasonal sustainable options – ask your local fishmonger if you're not sure what these are.

brown shrimps and spiced brown butter

Potted shrimps we all know and love. Adding spices (nutmeg, black pepper, bay and fennel seeds) to the caramelised brown butter makes this classic even more delicious in our opinion. Serve with toast or crispbread. Serves 4

150g unsalted butter
2 bay leaves (fresh if possible)
1 whole nutmeg, finely grated
pinch cayenne or hot paprika
½ teaspoon ground fennel seeds
¼ teaspoon ground black pepper
squeeze lemon juice
200g peeled brown shrimps
toast or crispbread, to serve

In a small pan, melt the butter with the bay leaves over a low heat. The butter will separate but continue to cook until the white milky bits of whey start to caramelise and turn golden. Now add the nutmeg, cayenne, fennel seeds and pepper, and cook for another minute or so, stirring occasionally to prevent anything sticking to the bottom of the pan.

Squeeze a little lemon juice over the shrimps and stir them into the butter. Season with salt, cook for 30 seconds, then scoop out the shrimps with a slotted spoon and transfer them to four small ramekins or one larger dish. Press them down with the back of the spoon, then pour over the warm butter and chill in the fridge for a couple of hours, until set. This can be done in advance.

ceviche with citrus salad and pistachios

We have included four ceviche recipes in this chapter as they are quick to assemble, light and refreshing. The marriage between citrus and fish is well known, and we especially like how the kaleidoscope of colours and flavours within the citrus family interact with the senses. Serves 4 as a starter

150-175g filleted skinless sea bass, bream or red mullet
juice ½ orange, ½ lime and ½ lemon
zest ¼ orange, ¼ lime and ¼ lemon
pinch dried oregano
8 segments each pink grapefruit, orange, lime and lemon,
    with peel, skin and pith removed
3 tablespoons chopped pistachios
extra virgin olive oil, to drizzle

At an angle of about 30° and using a sharp knife, slice the fish paper-thin (or flatten the slices slightly with the knife if not quite thin enough). Lay on one large or four small plates. Ideally do this in advance and leave to chill in the fridge, covered with parchment.

Mix the citrus juices and zests, oregano and a pinch of salt together.

Five minutes before you are ready to eat, spoon the citrus juices over – and a little bit under – the fish and leave to cure for 3-5 minutes.

Scatter the citrus segments and pistachios on top and drizzle with a little olive oil. Serve immediately.

Pictured on pages 172-3

ceviche with courgettes, lemon and basil

This is such a summery, light starter or lunch. We often use borage or marigold petals to enhance the beauty of the plate, but any other edible petals will do! Serves 4 as a starter

150–175g filleted skinless sea bass, bream or red mullet
300g small to medium courgettes, ideally ⅔ pale green and ⅓ yellow, topped and tailed
1 heaped teaspoon fine sea salt
4 tablespoons lemon juice and 2 tablespoons lime juice
zest ¼ lemon and ¼ lime
3 tablespoons basil leaves, roughly torn
2 tablespoons extra virgin olive oil + extra for drizzling
fennel fronds, borage or marigold petals (optional)

At an angle (about 30°) and using a sharp knife, slice the fish paper-thin (or flatten the slices slightly with the knife if not quite thin enough). Ideally do this in advance and leave to chill in the fridge, covered with parchment.

Slice the courgettes very thinly (1–2mm) with a sharp knife or with a mandolin. Place in a colander and toss well with the salt so the salt has a chance to 'cook' each slice. Leave for 20 minutes, then gently squeeze the courgettes to get rid of the excess water and transfer them to a large bowl along with the fish.

Mix the lemon and lime juice with the zest and a pinch of salt then pour over the courgettes and fish. Toss gently and leave for a couple of minutes. Add half the basil and the olive oil and toss again.

Spread the courgettes and fish on a plate and scatter over the remaining basil, fennel fronds or flower petals (if using) and an extra drizzle of olive oil. Serve immediately.

ceviche with pomegranates, lime and avocado

Alongside the lime, the tart juice of the pomegranate 'cooks' the fish but also adds gorgeous ruby tones to the plate, while the avocado provides a creamy softness in contrast to the sharpness. Serves 4 as a starter

150–175g filleted skinless sea bass, bream or tuna loin
3 tablespoons fresh pomegranate juice
3 tablespoons lime juice
zest ½ lime
4 heaped tablespoons diced avocado
3 tablespoons pomegranate seeds
2 tablespoons finely chopped mint
extra virgin olive oil, to drizzle

At an angle (about 30°) and using a sharp knife, slice the fish paper-thin (or flatten the slices slightly with the knife if not quite thin enough). Lay the fish on 1 large or 4 small plates. Ideally do this in advance and leave to chill in the fridge, covered with parchment.

Mix the pomegranate juice, lime juice and zest with a good pinch of salt.

Five minutes before you are ready to eat, spoon the dressing over – and a little bit under – the fish and leave to cure for 3–5 minutes.

Scatter the avocado, pomegranate seeds and mint on top, drizzle with olive oil and serve immediately.

ceviche with green apple and almond sauce

We had a variation of this dish at a tapas bar in Barcelona a few years ago. We love how well the shards of tart green apple and *ajo blanco* (almond and sherry vinegar sauce) go together. Serves 4 as a starter

150–175g filleted skinless sea bass, bream, or wild organic salmon
  or sea trout
3 tablespoons apple juice
3 tablespoons lime juice
2 Granny Smith apples, skin on, cored, sliced into thin matchsticks
1 heaped tablespoon finely shredded mint

Almond sauce
100g blanched almonds
10 tablespoons water
1½ tablespoons sherry vinegar + pinch sugar if not sweet
1 tablespoon extra virgin olive oil + extra for drizzling

To make the almond sauce, blitz the almonds in a food processor for a few minutes until as smooth as possible. With the machine still running, slowly add the water, then the sherry vinegar, olive oil and a pinch of salt. Transfer to a bowl, check for seasoning and set aside.

For the ceviche: at an angle (about 30°) and using a sharp knife, slice the fish paper-thin (or flatten the slices slightly with the knife if not quite thin enough) and lay on one large or four small plates. Ideally do this in advance and leave to chill in the fridge, covered with baking paper.

Mix the apple and lime juice with a pinch of salt. Five minutes before you are ready to eat, spoon the juice over – and a little bit under – the fish and leave to cure for 3–5 minutes.

To serve, spoon over the almond sauce then scatter over the apple matchsticks, mint and a drizzle of olive oil. Serve immediately.

squid and tomato salad with crispy capers

In the height of the tomato season, we use a mixture of red, yellow and green tomatoes. Though this is not essential, the flavour is everything. The squid is sliced super-thin, so it cooks in a matter of seconds when flashed in a hot pan. Salty, crispy capers add a delicate crunch and finish the dish well. Serves 4

6 tablespoons sunflower oil
3 tablespoons capers in brine, washed and squeezed dry
400g sweet cherry tomatoes, quartered
1 spring onion, finely sliced
1 teaspoon fresh oregano or marjoram or pinch dried
6 tablespoons extra virgin olive oil + extra for drizzling
2 tablespoons good-quality aged sweet red wine vinegar like cabernet sauvignon (page 303)
300g cleaned small to medium squid, sliced into thin strips 8cm x 0.5cm
3 tablespoons roughly chopped parsley

Heat the sunflower oil in a small saucepan over a medium heat and fry the capers until crisp, about 2 minutes. Transfer them using a slotted spoon onto kitchen paper to absorb any excess oil.

In a mixing bowl, combine the tomatoes, spring onion and oregano. Pour over 4 tablespoons olive oil and the vinegar, season and toss well.

Place a heavy frying pan over a high heat. Mix the squid with the remaining olive oil. When the pan is very hot, add the squid along with a pinch of salt and stir-fry for 30–40 seconds, stirring quickly until just cooked.

Transfer the squid to the tomato mix, toss once more and serve immediately, with the crispy capers, parsley and a drizzle of olive oil on top.

squid, potatoes, red wine and rosemary

This dish is inspired by two Greek recipes: octopus with red wine, and potatoes cooked with coriander seeds and red wine. Octopus is not that easy to source, so we thought squid would be more accessible. Red wine with fish seems odd but the wine reduces into a rich, savoury sauce that envelops the squid and potatoes. Serve with green goddess salad (page 91) or kale, preserved lemon and toasted almonds (page 79). Serves 4

6 tablespoons olive oil
1 banana shallot (60g), finely chopped
4 garlic cloves, thinly sliced
1 tablespoon roughly ground coriander seeds
1 tablespoon finely chopped rosemary
400g floury potatoes, cut into 4cm x 2cm wedges
400g cleaned small to medium squid, sliced into thin strips 4cm x 2cm
250ml medium red wine
1 tablespoon roughly chopped parsley
parsley and caper sauce to serve (page 256)

Place a large saucepan over a medium heat and when hot (but not too hot), add 5 tablespoons olive oil, the shallot and garlic. Fry for 3 minutes, until starting to turn golden.

Add the coriander seeds, rosemary and potatoes to the pan and stir well. Sauté the potatoes for about 5–6 minutes, stirring often, until golden, tender and slightly crisp.

Add the squid and stir to cook through for 1 minute. Add the wine, remaining olive oil and a pinch of salt. Simmer gently for 10 minutes with a tight-fitting lid on. Add a splash of water if needed and check for seasoning.

Serve with the parsley scattered on top and the parsley and caper sauce on the side.

squid kofte with *mojo verde*

Classic kofte is made with lamb. The idea for this lighter version came from a trendy tapas bar in San Sebastian that had *hamberguesita de choco* (mini cuttlefish burgers) on their menu. Samuel adapted it to a kofte by adding bulgur, coriander, chilli and cumin. You can use cuttlefish or squid. It is served with the Canarian green chilli salsa *mojo verde* and is delicious with either green goddess salad (page 91), chopped salad (page 94), fried potatoes with za'atar, peppers and feta (page 137), leek, pepper and walnut bulgur pilaf (page 153) or spinach and chickpeas (page 162). Serves 4

3 spring onions (white and green parts), trimmed and finely chopped
1 tablespoon olive oil + extra for frying the kofte
400g cleaned squid or cuttlefish (body and tentacles)
2 green chillies, deseeded and finely chopped
3 tablespoons fine bulgur, washed briefly in cold water and drained
  (if using larger bulgur, leave to soak in the water for 10 minutes)
2 teaspoons ground cumin seeds
3 tablespoons finely chopped coriander
lemon wedges, to serve

Mojo verde
25g coriander, leaves and stalks roughly chopped
4 tablespoons roughly chopped flat-leaf parsley
1 large green chilli or 2 small, deseeded if hot
1 small garlic clove
4 tablespoons extra virgin olive oil
1 tablespoon lemon juice

Fry the spring onions in the olive oil over a medium heat for 5–10 minutes, until soft and sweet. Set aside.

Cut the squid into pieces, then place in a food processor and blitz until finely chopped but still retaining some texture. Transfer the squid and the spring onions into a bowl and add the chillies, bulgur, cumin and coriander. Season with salt and pepper and mix well.

Place a large heavy frying pan over a medium to high heat and when hot add a few drops of oil. Take a dessertspoon of the kofte mixture and flatten to a disc about 6cm in diameter. Fill the pan with as many discs as you can, leaving gaps between them. Fry 45 seconds to 1 minute on each side, until lightly caramelised, then flip over with a spatula and fry the other side. Check for seasoning.

Put the *mojo verde* ingredients into a food processor and blitz until smooth. Season with salt. Serve with the kofte and lemon wedges on the side.

mussel and potato salad with paprika dressing

This recipe is inspired by the tinned seafood beloved by Spain and Portugal, and Basque garlic and paprika dressing served over grilled fish (our favourite restaurants to enjoy this are Kaia Kaipe or Elkano in Getaria). Green goddess salad (page 91), courgette salad without the Manchego (page 80), or spinach, pine nuts and sultanas (page 133) are the perfect accompaniment. Serves 4

300g small waxy potatoes, e.g. Pink Fir, Charlotte or Anya
50ml medium white wine
1kg mussels, cleaned, debearded and rinsed,
  discarding any that are open or broken
4 tablespoons olive oil
3 garlic cloves, thinly sliced
1–2 bird's-eye chillies, whole
1 teaspoon thyme leaves
2 bay leaves (optional)
3 tablespoons good-quality red wine vinegar like cabernet sauvignon
  (page 303) or sherry vinegar + pinch sugar if not sweet
1 teaspoon sweet (smoked) paprika
2 tablespoons very finely chopped shallot
3 tablespoons finely chopped parsley
½ tablespoon lemon juice

Boil the potatoes in salted water until tender, about 20 minutes. Drain and set aside to cool completely.

To cook the mussels, place a large saucepan over a high heat and add the white wine. When the wine is simmering, add the mussels, put a tight-fitting lid on the pan, and steam until the shells open. Set aside.

When cool enough to handle, remove the mussels from their shells. Taste the mussel juice for seasoning and set aside.

For the paprika dressing, place a small saucepan over a medium heat and add the olive oil, garlic, bird's-eye chillies, thyme and bay leaves (if using). Fry gently for 3–4 minutes, or until the garlic is golden brown all over, taking care that it does not burn as it will taste bitter. Remove from the heat and carefully add the vinegar, paprika and black pepper. Add 1 tablespoon mussel juice to the paprika oil and check for seasoning.

To serve, peel and slice the cooled potatoes into 1cm rounds and place them in a bowl with the mussels, shallot and parsley. Pour over the dressing and lemon juice, toss gently and serve.

mussels with yoghurt, dill and crispy chickpeas

The mussels here are paired with yoghurt rather than cream, so this is a little sharper than moules marinière, but the idea is similar. Crispy chickpeas are for texture. Partner with homemade chips or fried courgettes with *cacık* (page 114). Serves 4

6 tablespoons olive oil
100g tinned chickpeas, patted dry with a clean tea towel
3 garlic cloves, thinly sliced
1kg mussels, cleaned, debearded and rinsed,
   discarding any that are open or broken
50ml white wine
pinch saffron
5 tablespoons chopped dill
6 tablespoons full-fat plain yoghurt, mixed with 1 egg yolk
   and ½ teaspoon baharat or allspice

For the chickpeas, add 2 tablespoons olive oil to a small frying pan over a medium heat. Once hot, but not smoking, add the chickpeas and fry for 7–8 minutes, until golden and crisp. Remove from the heat and transfer the chickpeas onto kitchen paper using a slotted spoon to absorb excess oil. Keep warm.

For the mussels, place a large saucepan over a medium to high heat. When hot, add the remaining olive oil and the garlic and fry for 30 seconds, or until the garlic starts to turn golden. Add the mussels, stir well, and bring up to temperature again. Add the wine, saffron and half the dill, stir well, then put a lid on the pan and steam until the shells open.

With a large slotted spoon, transfer the mussels to a dish and keep warm. Whisk the yoghurt mixture into the mussel juices and simmer for 1–2 minutes, to thicken. Stir in the remaining dill, check for seasoning, then pour the yoghurt over the mussels and sprinkle over the crispy chickpeas.

* TORTILLITAS DE CAMARÓN..... 3.00€
* ZAMBURIÑAS... 3.50€
* BACALAO A LA PLANCHA... 3.50€
* GAMBITAS FRITAS... 3.00€

* PULPO A LA BRASA... 14.00€

BAR
EL ATÚN

81 PESCADOS

clams, white wine and coriander

Clams with white wine and coriander is a classic Portugese dish. We often jump over the border into Portugal and love the culture shock of two countries that are similar in so many ways, yet so different. Serve with lots of good bread to soak up the juices. Serves 4

8 tablespoons olive oil
2 garlic cloves, thinly sliced
2 teaspoons lightly crushed coriander seeds
pinch of crumbled dried chilli or chilli flakes
4 bay leaves (fresh if possible)
1kg small clams, e.g. venus or palourdes, rinsed thoroughly,
   discarding any that are broken or open
150ml good-quality medium white wine
6 tablespoons finely chopped coriander leaves
bread and lemon wedges, to serve

Place a large saucepan over a medium heat. Add 6 tablespoons olive oil, and when hot, but not smoking, add the garlic, coriander seeds, chilli and bay leaves. Fry for 30 seconds, or until the garlic starts to turn golden, then increase the temperature to high and stir in the clams.

Add the wine and half the coriander leaves, stir well, then put a lid on the pan for 2–4 minutes, until the shells steam open.

Add the remaining coriander and olive oil, check for seasoning. Serve with the lemon wedges on the side and lots of bread to mop up the juices.

clams, white wine and asparagus

Add asparagus to the clams for variety. If the asparagus is thick we peel it lengthways to create shavings that we add a couple of minutes before the end. Serves 4

8–10 thick green asparagus spears, woody ends snapped off
8 tablespoons olive oil
3 garlic cloves, thinly sliced
1 teaspoon thyme leaves
3 bay leaves (fresh if possible)
1kg small clams, e.g. venus or palourdes, rinsed thoroughly,
   discarding any that are broken or open
150ml good-quality medium white wine
bread, to serve

Cut the tips off the asparagus, cut in half lengthways and set aside. To make the asparagus strips, lay the spears on a chopping board and use a vegetable peeler to peel from the bottom to the top of the spears, applying downward pressure as you do so.

Add 6 tablespoons olive oil to a large saucepan over a medium heat, and when hot, but not smoking, add the garlic, thyme and bay leaves. Fry for 30 seconds, or until the garlic starts to turn golden, then increase the temperature to high and stir in the clams. Add the wine and asparagus strips without stirring, then put a lid on the pan for 2-3 minutes, until the shells steam open and the asparagus is tender.

Stir well, add the remaining oil, check for seasoning and serve with bread to mop up the juices.

scallops with Albariño wine

Thankfully, the wine needed in the ingredients is minimal, so there is more for the glass! Serve on its own as a starter or with courgette, lemon and basil salad without the Manchego (page 80), peas with jamón and mint (page 139), gem lettuce, peas and pancetta (page 117) or roast squash with sweet vinegar, garlic and rosemary (page 118). Serves 4

75g butter
3 spring onions (white and green parts), finely chopped
2 teaspoons thyme leaves
8 medium to large scallops, cleaned and with the coral still attached,
    preferably with 8 half shells
1 bottle Albariño wine
bread, to serve

Preheat the oven to 220°C/425°F/gas 7.

While the oven is coming up to temperature, place a medium saucepan over a medium heat and add the butter. When it starts to foam, add the spring onions, thyme leaves and a pinch of salt. Cook for 4 minutes, stirring occasionally, until the onions are sweet and lightly caramelised. Set aside.

Place the scallops (in their shells) in a large roasting tray. Spoon 2 teaspoons of the buttery spring onion mixture, followed by 1 tablespoon Albariño wine onto each scallop. Season with salt and pepper. If you don't have scallop shells, simply place the scallops in a hot ovenproof dish and continue as before. Roast for 8-10 minutes in the hot oven, and serve immediately, with bread and glasses of chilled Albariño.

scallops, roast asparagus and thyme dressing

The thyme dressing brings everything together in this dish. At Moro we chop up the corals into two or three pieces so that we have bright-orange nuggets to scatter over as a garnish. This is delicious with lentils, peas, asparagus and broad beans (page 158) or lentils and chorizo (page 165). Serves 4

20-30 (depending on thickness) green asparagus spears,
   woody ends snapped off
3 tablespoons extra virgin olive oil
8 medium to large scallops, cleaned, corals separated from
   the white meat and cut into thirds

Thyme dressing
4 tablespoons lemon thyme
½ garlic clove, crushed with salt
5 tablespoons extra virgin olive oil
1 tablespoon lemon juice

Preheat the oven to 220°C/425°F/gas 7.

Make the thyme dressing while the oven is heating up. Put the thyme leaves into a pestle and mortar or food processor with the garlic and a good pinch of salt and pound or blitz to a paste. Very gradually drizzle in 5 tablespoons olive oil. Transfer to a bowl and stir in the lemon juice. Check for seasoning and set aside.

Place the asparagus in a bowl, add 2 tablespoons olive oil, season with salt and pepper and toss until the asparagus is coated. Transfer to an oiled roasting tray and roast for 8-10 minutes, depending on thickness, until wilted and golden.

Heat a large heavy frying pan over a medium to high heat. Rub the remaining olive oil over the scallops, season with salt and pepper, and add both white meat and orange corals to the hot pan. Sear for 1 minute on each side, or until lightly caramelised.

Arrange the warm asparagus randomly on plates, then place the scallops in the gaps and spoon over the thyme dressing.

sea bass with migas, lemon zest, garlic and parsley

The lemon zest, garlic and parsley (gremolada) lifts the migas. For a light accompaniment, try the autumn salad (page 85), beetroot, apple and mint salad (page 95), spinach, pine nuts and sultanas (page 133), lentils, peas, asparagus and broad beans (page 158) or spinach and chickpeas (page 162). Serves 4

4 sea bass fillets, approximately 170g each (or any other white fish you fancy)
2 tablespoons extra virgin olive oil
lemon wedges, to serve

Migas
½ loaf ciabatta, crusts removed, cut into 2cm cubes
2 tablespoons extra virgin olive oil
2 garlic cloves, finely chopped
zest 2 lemons
2 tablespoons finely chopped flat-leaf parsley

Heat the oven to 200°C/400°F/gas 6.

Place the ciabatta in a large roasting tin, toss with 2 tablespoons olive oil and season with salt. Bake in the oven for 8–10 minutes, until golden and crisp but not too hard. Remove from the heat and set aside to cool.

When cool, crush the baked bread to make slightly uneven breadcrumbs and put them into a bowl with the garlic, zest and parsley.

Place a large frying pan over a medium heat and when hot add the remaining olive oil. Season the sea bass fillets and pan-fry over a medium heat on both sides until just cooked.

Transfer to a serving dish and generously sprinkle the migas on top.
Serve with extra lemon if you wish.

turbot with anchovy, rosemary and paprika butter

This anchovy butter is so good and so versatile as it is also excellent on lamb, asparagus or simply a piece of toast! It is better to make it in advance. The recipe here is for double the quantity that you will need for this dish, but you will be pleased to have extra in the fridge and it will happily last a week or two. Serves 4

4 turbot tranches (on the bone), about 180-200g each and 3cm thick
extra virgin olive oil

Anchovy, rosemary and paprika butter
50g good-quality salted anchovies (we use Ortiz, page 304), drained
2 heaped tablespoons very finely chopped rosemary
1 tablespoon lemon juice
200g good-quality unsalted butter, slightly soft
1 teaspoon sweet smoked paprika

For the butter, place the anchovies, rosemary and lemon juice in a food processor and blitz until smooth. Add the butter and paprika, season with black pepper and blitz further until smooth. Check for balance between the ingredients, and for salt. Transfer to a bowl, refrigerate until a bit firmer, then shape into a cylinder, wrap in clingfilm and chill, preferably overnight, until firm.

Half an hour before you are ready to eat, heat the oven to 200°C/400°F/gas 6.

Place a heavy ovenproof frying pan over a medium to high heat. Rub the turbot tranches liberally with olive oil and season with rock salt and pepper. Fry for 3-5 minutes, until golden on one side, then turn them over and fry for 1 more minute. Transfer the tranches to the oven for another 5-10 minutes, or until cooked through.

Serve with a generous slice of the anchovy butter on top of each tranche alongside some braised spinach or salad and new potatoes.

sea bass baked with fig leaves and walnut sauce

There are surprisingly more fig trees in the UK than you would imagine. The leaves impart a wonderful exotic aroma into the fish. They fall in the autumn, so try this dish between May and early October, or you can pick and freeze fig leaves. Lemon or kaffir lime leaves from Asian supermarkets, which you can buy online, are a good alternative, but you will need triple the quantity. This dish is delicious with the leek, pepper and walnut bulgur pilaf (page 153). Serves 4

100g walnuts
2 tablespoons roughly chopped coriander
½ teaspoon crushed coriander seeds
1 garlic clove
1 tablespoon good-quality sweet red wine vinegar like cabernet sauvignon
  or moscatel vinegar (page 303)
½ teaspoon sugar
6 tablespoons extra virgin olive oil
1 large whole sea bass or 2–4 mackerel or bream,
  gutted and seasoned with salt and pepper
8–12 large fig leaves, stalks removed
lemon wedges, to serve

Preheat the oven to 200°C/400°F/gas 6.

For the walnut sauce, put the walnuts, coriander, coriander seeds, garlic, red wine vinegar, sugar, olive oil and a good pinch of salt and pepper into a food processor and blitz well. Add enough water to loosen the walnuts, until the sauce is almost smooth and the consistency of thick double cream. Transfer to a bowl and check for seasoning.

Line a large roasting tin or dish with the fig leaves, and lay the fish on top. Cover the fish with more leaves, tucking them under the sides like a blanket, then wrap in foil to secure the leaves. Roast in the oven for 20–40 minutes depending on the size of the fish or grill over charcoal on very low embers until cooked through.

Serve with the walnut sauce on the side and wedges of lemon.

Pictured on pages 206-7

fried monkfish with lemon, garlic, coriander and dill

This recipe comes from Uzbekistan - fish is coated in flour, fried in olive oil, then doused straightaway with lemon juice seasoned with crushed raw garlic, and showered with lots of fresh dill, coriander and red chilli. This is delicious with spinach and chickpeas (page 162), fried potatoes with za'atar, peppers and feta (page 137) or cucumber, tahini sauce and chilli (page 83). Serves 4

900g monkfish or hake on the bone, cut across into 2.5cm slices
2 garlic cloves, grated
4 tablespoons lemon juice
zest 1 lemon
2 tablespoons lime juice
4 tablespoons water
8 tablespoons olive oil
5 tablespoons plain flour, seasoned with salt and pepper
6 tablespoons roughly chopped coriander
6 tablespoons roughly chopped dill
2 long red chillies, halved lengthways and sliced across very thinly
lemon or lime wedges, to serve

Twenty minutes before cooking, sprinkle the fish generously with salt all over and leave for 5-10 minutes.

Mix the garlic with the lemon juice, lemon zest, lime juice and water, and season with a little salt.

When you are ready to fry the fish, heat the oil in a large high-sided saucepan until very hot, but not smoking. Lightly dust the fish with the seasoned flour on all sides, tapping off any excess. Fry the fish for 5 minutes (be careful not to overcrowd the pan; fry in batches if necessary) on the first side and 2 minutes on the second, until golden brown. Remove from the oil with a slotted spoon and briefly drain on kitchen paper to absorb any excess oil.

Transfer to a serving plate, lightly douse in the dressing and sprinkle with the coriander, dill and chilli. Serve with lemon or lime wedges.

mackerel with tomato, olive and sherry vinaigrette

We make an emulsified vinaigrette with sherry vinegar, so it is served as a sauce for the tomatoes more than as a dressing, and it cuts through the oily flesh of the mackerel. Serves 4

3 teaspoons Dijon mustard
7 tablespoons extra virgin olive oil
4 teaspoons sherry vinegar + pinch sugar if not sweet
3 tablespoons finely shredded basil
4 mackerel fillets, seasoned with salt and pepper
3 ripe vine tomatoes (300g), blanched in boiling water to remove the skins, deseeded and finely chopped
2 tablespoons finely chopped black olives

For the sherry vinaigrette, put the mustard into a small bowl and whisk in 5 tablespoons olive oil, then the sherry vinegar. Stir in the basil, set aside.

Place a large frying pan over a high heat and add the remaining olive oil. When the oil is hot, but not smoking, add the fillets, flesh side down (in two batches if not enough room). Fry for 1–2 minutes until caramelised, then turn over for another minute or so. When just cooked, transfer to a plate.

Mix the chopped tomatoes and olives with the sherry vinaigrette and spoon over the fish. Serve immediately.

tuna with fennel seeds, oregano and chilli

The fennel, oregano and chilli are really used as a seasoning in this dish. Most salads or vegetables are compatible accompaniments, and you don't need to use tuna, any fish will suffice. Serves 4

1 tablespoon olive oil
4 tuna steaks
2 heaped teaspoons whole fennel seeds
1 teaspoon fresh or dried oregano
1–2 red chillies, cut in half lengthways, deseeded and finely chopped
lemon wedges, to serve

Place a large frying pan over a high heat. Drizzle the oil over the tuna and rub all over. Sprinkle the fennel and oregano on both sides and season well with salt and pepper.

When the pan is hot, add the tuna and sear briefly for about 30–60 seconds on both sides, depending on how rare you like it and the thickness of the steak. Transfer immediately to a plate, sprinkle over the chilli.

Serve with the lemon wedges and a sauce, such as parsley and caper sauce (page 256), chilli and coriander salsa (page 44) or *mojo verde* (page 184).

easy meat

Like fish, animals are precious. Our diet requires much less protein than you think, so enjoy meat as a treat rather than the norm, and always source responsibly.

chicken liver pâté
with Oloroso sherry

A glass of Matusalem cream by Gonzalez Byass is wonderful with this!
This dish can be prepared a day ahead. Lots of toast and sips of sherry
are essential to the overall experience. Serves 4

220g unsalted butter, cut into cubes
1 banana shallot (60g), very finely chopped
1 tablespoon thyme leaves
400g organic chicken livers, trimmed of all fat and sinew and rinsed very well
    under cold water until the water runs clear
70ml Oloroso dulce (sweet Oloroso sherry), cream sherry or brandy

Heat 25g butter in a large stainless steel, non-reactive frying pan over
a medium heat. When the butter begins to foam, add the shallot, thyme,
a pinch of salt and cook for 5 minutes, stirring occasionally, until the shallot
is sweet and caramelised. Remove from the pan and set aside.

Drain the livers well and pat dry. Add another 50g butter to the pan and
when very hot, season the livers with salt and pepper and sear on one
side for 1 minute, turn, then add the shallot mixture, season and fry for
another minute. Add the sherry and simmer for another minute, then turn
the livers again.

Remove from the heat, transfer to a bowl to cool before transferring to
a food processor with 75g unmelted butter. Blitz until smooth. Check for
seasoning, then transfer the mixture to a small dish or four ramekins. Melt
the final 70g butter and pour over the top. Place in the fridge to set for a
couple of hours. The pâté will keep for a few days.

chicken livers, baharat and pomegranate molasses

Baharat is a Middle Eastern spice blend of paprika, coriander, black pepper, cumin, cinnamon, cayenne, cloves, nutmeg and cardamom, or variations on that theme. One large pomegranate should suffice for the juice and seeds needed here. Serve this with Greek yoghurt and warm pitta or flatbread. Serves 4

25g unsalted butter
1 banana shallot, very finely chopped
400–500g organic chicken livers, trimmed of all fat and sinew,
    and rinsed very well under cold water until the water runs clear
1 tablespoon olive oil + extra for drizzling
¾ teaspoon baharat
3 tablespoons pomegranate molasses
4 tablespoons fresh pomegranate juice
250g strained Greek yoghurt, seasoned with a little salt
3 tablespoons pomegranate seeds
2 tablespoons finely shredded mint
flatbreads or pittas, warmed

Heat the butter in a large frying pan over a low to medium heat. When the butter begins to foam, add the shallot and a pinch of salt and cook for 5–8 minutes, stirring occasionally, until sweet and caramelised. Remove from the pan and set aside.

Drain the livers well and pat dry. Add the olive oil to the pan, season the livers with salt and the baharat, and when the oil is very hot, add them to the pan. Fry for a minute, until sealed and browned on one side, then turn them over and fry for another minute.

Stir in the shallot, pomegranate molasses and juice, and fry for another 30–60 seconds – the livers should still be pink and soft in the middle. Check for seasoning.

Spread out the yoghurt on a plate and spoon the livers on top. Add the pomegranate seeds, mint and an extra drizzle of olive oil to finish. Serve with warm flatbreads or pittas on the side.

chicken salad with orange, grapefruit, mint and pistachio sauce

A refreshing, light salad that is ideal if you have some leftover roast chicken.
Serves 4

2 tablespoons olive oil
400–450g organic or free-range chicken fillets (2 per person)
   or leftover roast chicken
½ teaspoon ground cinnamon
2 baby gems, trimmed, outer leaves removed, cut lengthways into thin wedges
2 chicory (red or white), chopped across into 3cm pieces
6 tablespoons mint leaves
½ tablespoon chopped chives
1 pink grapefruit, skin and pith removed, segmented
1 large orange, skin and pith removed, segmented
1 teaspoon chopped red chilli

Lime dressing
4 tablespoons extra virgin olive oil
juice 1 lime, seasoned with good pinch salt and sugar

Pistachio sauce
juice 2 limes
100g pistachios, roughly ground, some fine
3 tablespoons extra virgin olive oil
1 teaspoon sugar

For the pistachio sauce, combine all the ingredients and season with salt and pepper. Thin with a little water if necessary. Set aside.

For the lime dressing, whisk the ingredients together and set aside.

To cook the chicken, place a large frying pan over a high heat. When hot, add 1 tablespoon olive oil. Season the chicken fillets with salt and a sprinkling of cinnamon, and add half to the pan. Fry for 2–2½ minutes on each side, remove from the pan and keep warm while you fry the rest. Tear into bite-sized chunks.

Put the salad, mint leaves, chives, grapefruit and orange into a large bowl.

To serve, pour the dressing over the salad, add the chicken and any juices, season and toss. Drizzle over the pistachio sauce and sprinkle with chilli.

roast chicken with two marinades

Two different marinades for roast chicken. The fenugreek and coriander marinade goes well with spiced labneh, tomatoes, mint and dukkah (page 68), the fennel seed, garlic and thyme marinade goes well with labneh, mushrooms, sweet herbs and chilli butter (page 67) and most of the salad and vegetables dishes in this book are compatible. You could also ask the butcher to bone and spatchcock the chicken, then grill it over low embers on a barbecue. Serves 4-6

1 x 1.5-1.7kg organic chicken

Fennel seed, garlic and thyme marinade
3 garlic cloves
½ teaspoon salt
4 teaspoons roughly ground fennel seeds
3 tablespoons thyme leaves
2 tablespoons olive oil + extra for drizzling
1 tablespoon lemon juice

Fenugreek and coriander marinade
3 garlic cloves
½ teaspoon salt
2 teaspoons roughly ground coriander seeds
2 teaspoons ground fenugreek
1 teaspoon ground cumin seeds
1 tablespoon thyme leaves
½ teaspoon Aleppo chilli flakes (page 304)
5 cherry tomatoes
2 tablespoons olive oil + extra for drizzling

Either flatten the chicken by boning it through the backbone and removing the carcass and thigh bones, or ask your butcher to do it for you. Or, for greater ease, roast the bird whole! Use either of the marinades above.

For each marinade, blitz all the ingredients in a food processor until smooth. Rub the chosen marinade over both the flesh and skin side of the chicken. Prise some of the skin from the breast meat and push some of the marinade into these small pockets. Ideally marinate the chicken 2-12 hours in advance.

Preheat the oven to 200°C/400°F/gas 6. Place the chicken on a lightly oiled roasting tray, drizzle with a little olive oil, season, then roast for 1-1¼ hours if whole or 30-40 minutes if boned, just until the meat juices run clear. Transfer to a board and rest for 10-15 minutes, loosely covered with foil. Return any juices back to the roasting tin and deglaze with a splash of water. Slice the chicken and serve with the fragrant gravy on top.

chicken with preserved lemon labneh

Adding preserved lemon to labneh or yoghurt works really well. To simplify things, serve it with roast chicken. This is excellent with green goddess salad (page 91), courgette salad (page 80), kale and preserved lemon (page 79) or lentils, peas, asparagus and broad beans (page 158). Serves 4

4 skinless, boneless organic chicken breasts
100g plain flour, seasoned with good pinch salt
2 free-range or organic eggs, lightly beaten
150g fresh, seasoned breadcrumbs
lemon wedges, to serve

Preserved lemon labneh
250g Greek yoghurt
75g cream cheese
3 garlic cloves, crushed with a little sea salt
2 tablespoons finely chopped preserved lemon rind (page 303)
zest 2 lemons
2 teaspoons nigella seeds
1 green chilli, finely chopped

To make the preserved lemon labneh, mix all the ingredients together and check for seasoning. Scoop 4 separate heaped tablespoons onto a plate and freeze for at least 2 hours (longer if you have the time).

Preheat the oven to 180°C/350°F/gas 4. Place the chicken breasts on a chopping board. Using a sharp knife, slice through each breast parallel to your board to make a deep pocket, being careful not to cut all the way through. Tuck the frozen labneh into the pockets, pushing it in as far as possible before tucking the breast around it to seal in the labneh.

Put the seasoned flour into a shallow bowl, the whisked eggs into another, and the breadcrumbs into a third. Lightly and evenly coat each chicken breast in the seasoned flour, patting off any excess. Then coat with the egg, letting any excess drip off. Finally, coat with the breadcrumbs.

Place on a lightly oiled baking tray and bake for 30–40 minutes, until the breadcrumbs are crisp and the chicken is cooked through (75°C at the thickest part). Cooking time will depend on the size of the breasts, so do check. Serve alongside lemon wedges and the rest of the labneh on the side.

Pictured on pages 224-5

duck breasts with walnut and pomegranate sauce

This is an adaptation of a classic Persian stew with walnuts and pomegranates called *fesenjān*. Instead of chicken, we have used duck breasts and made the sauce to spoon over the duck rather than being slowly braised in it. This is delicious with spinach, pine nuts and sultanas (page 133), spiced potato cake (page 104), salad or brown rice and potato pilaf (page 149). Serves 4

3-4 duck breasts (140-150g each, not too thick)
1 tablespoon olive oil
1 teaspoon fine salt
½ teaspoon ground cinnamon
50g butter
4 spring onions (white and green parts), finely chopped
¼ teaspoon ground turmeric
¼ teaspoon ground allspice, baharat or cinnamon
100g walnuts, very finely ground
2 tablespoons pomegranate molasses
300ml fresh pomegranate juice
4 tablespoons pomegranate seeds

Preheat the oven to 200°C/400°F/gas 6.

Cutting criss-cross on the skin of the duck breasts using a very sharp knife, rub them all over with the oil and sprinkle them with the salt and cinnamon. Set aside.

In a medium saucepan, melt the butter over a medium heat and as it begins to foam, add the spring onions, turmeric, allspice and a pinch of salt and stir well. Sauté for 5 minutes, stirring occasionally, until soft and sweet, then stir in the walnuts, pomegranate molasses and juice, and simmer gently for 10 minutes, stirring occasionally. Check for seasoning.

Meanwhile, place a heavy ovenproof frying pan over a medium to low heat and when hot, add the duck breasts skin side down. Fry for 3-5 minutes, until golden brown and crisp, then turn over and cook for another 3 minutes. Transfer to the oven another 5-6 minutes to finish, until pink, then remove and leave to rest on a plate covered with foil for 5 minutes. Add the duck juices to the warm sauce.

To serve, divide the sauce between four plates, slice the breasts on an angle, lay on top of the sauce, and scatter over the pomegranate seeds.

pork fillet with roast peppers

At Moro we often use ibérico pork from the exceptional black Iberian breed of pig that produces a dark and heavily marbled meat that produces an excellent flavour. You can source this in supermarkets or online, but of course free-range or organic pork is wonderful too. Spinach and chickpeas (page 162), brown rice and potato pilaf (page 149), or spiced potato cake (page 104) work well with this. If you can barbecue the peppers and pork over charcoal, even better! Serves 4

4 red romero or bell peppers
4 tablespoons olive oil
1 tablespoon sweet red wine vinegar like cabernet sauvignon or
   sherry vinegar (page 303)
1 tablespoon finely chopped rosemary or thyme
400–500g ibérico pork loin, presa or secreto, or pork tenderloin fillets,
   in slices 1cm thick
parsley and caper sauce (page 256)
lemon wedges, to serve

Preheat the oven to 220°C/425°F/gas 7.

Place the whole peppers on a roasting tray and drizzle them with a little olive oil. Roast for 45 minutes, until collapsed and blackened in places, then remove from the oven and allow to cool.

Peel away the skin from the cooled peppers and remove the seeds. Tear the peppers into strips and put them into a bowl with 2 tablespoons of the olive oil and vinegar. Season with salt and black pepper, then set aside.

When you are ready to cook the pork, rub the remaining oil, rosemary or thyme and plenty of salt and pepper all over the meat. Place a large heavy frying pan or griddle over a high heat. When hot, add the pork and fry on one side for 2–3 minutes, until light brown and caramelised, then turn over and cook for another 1–2 minutes. Remove from the heat and rest for 2 minutes.

Serve the pork with the peppers and parsley and caper sauce on the side. Also delicious with rosemary dressing (page 233).

Pictured on pages 230–31

veal escalopes, rosemary and jamón

This rosemary dressing is one of our favourite sauces. We often make double the quantity and keep the rest in the fridge as it lasts up to a week and can make a simple ingredient taste exquisite. Lentils, peas, asparagus and broad beans (page 158) or spiced potato cake (page 104) and a salad would go well with this. Serves 4

40g butter
300g free-range or organic rose veal or chicken escalopes or pork fillet, 75g per portion, sliced 0.5cm thick (if using pork fillet, flatten to 0.5cm and slice across at 1cm intervals)
4 slices jamón ibérico or jamón serrano (page 303)
lemon wedges, to serve

Rosemary dressing
3 tablespoons very finely chopped rosemary
1 tablespoon lemon juice
3 tablespoons extra virgin olive oil

For the rosemary dressing, in a pestle and mortar or a food processor, pound or blitz the rosemary until smooth. Add the lemon juice, then pound or blitz again until smooth. Slowly add the olive oil and salt to taste. Set aside.

Place a large heavy frying pan over a high heat. Add the butter and, when foaming vigorously (but not burning), add the veal (or chicken or pork). Sear for 45 seconds, depending on thickness, then turn over and fry for another 45 seconds until golden but still juicy and pink inside (longer for chicken or pork). Remove from the heat, transfer to a warm plate and rest for 30 seconds.

Spoon over the rosemary dressing and lay the jamón on top. Serve with lemon wedges.

seared beef with blue cheese sauce and roast mushrooms

The Picos de Europa mountains in the northern Spanish province of Asturias are home to the wonderful Cabrales and Picos blue cheeses. Local to that region is a dish of grilled beef with a simple blue cheese and cream sauce. Serves 4

4 sirloin or rib-eye steaks (150–250g each)
40g unsalted butter
2 garlic cloves, finely chopped
1 tablespoon finely chopped parsley
4 large flat field or Portobello mushrooms, peeled
2 tablespoons olive oil
150ml double cream
1 tablespoon fresh thyme leaves
1 teaspoon freshly grated nutmeg
100–125g Picos blue, Cabrales, Stilton, Saint Agur or Roquefort cheese,
    to taste, rind removed, crumbled
watercress, to serve

Take the beef out of the fridge at least an hour before grilling to bring it up to room temperature.

Preheat the oven to 200°C/400°F/gas 6. Mix the butter, garlic and parsley together. Place the mushrooms, gill side up, into an oiled roasting tin or dish and place a knob of the garlic butter on top of each mushroom. Drizzle with a little olive oil, season with salt and pepper and roast for 15–20 minutes.

While the mushrooms are in the oven, warm the cream over a low to medium heat, add the thyme, nutmeg and cheese, season with black pepper and stir gently to melt the cheese. When the cheese is almost melted, remove from the heat and set aside.

Ensure your grill, griddle pan or barbecue is very hot. Just before cooking, season the steaks well with sea salt and black pepper. Don't use oil – if the grill or pan is hot enough, it won't stick. Sear for a couple of minutes to get a good colour, then turn. Keep turning regularly to avoid burning. Cook for medium-rare, 4–6 minutes (55°C– 60°C); medium, 6–8 minutes (60°C– 65°C); medium-well 8–10 minutes. The beef should be soft and yielding still to touch. Rest it on a warm plate for 10 minutes.

Serve with the sauce on top, the mushrooms on the side and some watercress.

roast shoulder of pork marinated with orange and cumin

This really is a delicious way to cook pork shoulder. It is slow-roasted until the meat is soft and tender and the marinade has turned into a gravy delicately flavoured with orange and cumin. We recommend spinach, pine nuts and sultanas (page 133) and some fried potatoes to go with it. Serves 4

1 boneless pork shoulder, 1.2–3kg

Marinade
100ml orange juice
zest 1 orange, finely grated
2 rounded teaspoons roughly ground cumin seeds
1 tablespoon white wine vinegar
½ teaspoon smoked sweet paprika (page 304)
¼ teaspoon hot paprika
pinch saffron
1 small onion or banana shallot

Blitz all the marinade ingredients together in a food processor or with a hand blender and season with salt. Smear the marinade all over the meat and leave for a minimum of 30 minutes or overnight.

Preheat the oven to 190°C/375°F/gas 5.

When you are ready to roast the meat, wrap it tightly in tin foil and place it on a roasting tray. Slow-roast for 3 hours, then remove from the oven and let it rest for 20 minutes.

When you take off the foil, take care to keep all the juices from the marinade. Slice the meat and spoon over the juices.

lamb chops three ways

Lamb chops are super quick and these three ways of serving them are also super easy. Serve with any sides you wish. Serves 4–6

8–12 lamb chops

Marinade
4 garlic cloves, crushed to a paste with a little salt
1 small onion, finely grated
1 teaspoon paprika
4 teaspoons ground cumin seeds
4 tablespoons lemon juice
4 tablespoons olive oil

Mix the marinade ingredients together and smother all over the chops. Leave to marinate for 1 hour to overnight.

Season the chops with salt and pepper and place under a hot grill or on a barbecue or griddle pan. Cook for 3–4 minutes on each side, depending on the thickness and how cooked you like them. Rest for 5 minutes. Serve with one of the variations opposite.

Cumin and paprika
1 tablespoon ground cumin seeds
1 teaspoon sweet (smoked) paprika (page 304)
1 teaspoon Aleppo chilli flakes (page 304)
2 teaspoons Maldon salt
lemon wedges, to serve

Combine all the ingredients except the lemon and sprinkle over the chops just before serving with the lemon wedges.

Anchovy, rosemary and paprika butter
anchovy, rosemary and paprika butter (page 204)
2 tablespoons roughly chopped mint
lemon wedges, to serve

Follow the recipe for the anchovy, rosemary and paprika butter on page 204. Smear a slice of butter on top of each chop, sprinkle with the chopped mint and serve with lemon wedges.

Hot mint sauce
3 tablespoons olive oil
3 garlic cloves, thinly sliced
1 teaspoon cumin seeds
2 tablespoons good-quality red wine vinegar like cabernet sauvignon (page 303)
½ teaspoon sugar
4 tablespoons finely shredded mint

Place a small saucepan over a medium heat and add the olive oil. When hot, add the garlic and cumin seeds and fry gently until the garlic is golden. Add the vinegar, sugar and a pinch of salt then simmer for 20 seconds. Remove from the heat, stir in the mint and check for seasoning. Spoon over the chops and serve.

maghrebi slow-roast shoulder of lamb

We slow-roast the lamb shoulder until tender so that it can be shredded with a fork. This is delicious with roast squash (pages 118 and 249), roast red onions and beetroot with pomegranates (page 134) or one of the pilafs (pages 149 and 153) and some labneh on the side (page 37). You could also make kebabs with the leftovers and chopped salad (page 94), yoghurt and pitta. Serves 4

1.6–1.8kg shoulder of lamb, trimmed of any excess fat
1 garlic clove, thinly sliced
100g butter, softened
1 rounded tablespoon baharat
1 tablespoon very finely chopped or blitzed preserved lemon rind
  (page 303)
juice ½ lemon, to deglaze the pan
3 tablespoons whole coriander leaves

Preheat the oven to 220°C/425°F/gas 7.

Make a few small incisions into the lamb and slide in the garlic. Mix the butter with the baharat and preserved lemon rind. Rub this all over the lamb and season with salt and black pepper.

Place the lamb in a roasting tin and cover with foil. Turn the oven down to 160°C/325°F/gas 3 and roast the lamb for 3½–4 hours. Baste the meat every 45 minutes. The lamb is ready when the meat is very soft and easily falls away from the bone.

Remove the lamb from the oven and rest on a board for a good 20–30 minutes, covered with some foil. Pour off the excess fat from the roasting tin and loosen the juices with a little boiling water and a squeeze of lemon. Check for seasoning. Serve the lamb with the gravy, and the coriander leaves on top.

PRODUCIDO EN ESPAÑA

easy one-pot

The aim of this chapter is to simplify complex cooking methods and minimise on the washing-up. You don't need a side for these recipes, though a simple green salad and some bread is always welcome.

roast squash, peppers, chickpeas and herby yoghurt

This is delicious with fish or chicken, like roast chicken with fenugreek and coriander marinade (page 222). Serves 4

800g butternut squash, peeled, deseeded and cut into 3cm cubes
2 red romero or bell peppers, cut in half, deseeded and cut into 3cm pieces
1 garlic clove, crushed with a little salt
1 teaspoon ground cinnamon
2 tablespoons olive oil
1 x 400g tin cooked chickpeas, drained
50ml water
½ small red onion, finely chopped

Herby yoghurt
3 tablespoons each roughly chopped basil, dill, tarragon and parsley
1 tablespoon roughly chopped mint
½ garlic clove, crushed with a little salt
150g Greek yoghurt
1 tablespoon tahini
2 tablespoons extra virgin olive oil
squeeze lemon juice

Preheat the oven to 200°C/400°F/gas 6.

Toss the squash and peppers with the garlic, cinnamon, olive oil, salt and pepper. Place on a roasting tray and roast for 30–35 minutes, until soft and caramelised.

Meanwhile make the herby yoghurt by blitzing all the ingredients together with a hand blender or in a food processor. Season to taste.

Place the chickpeas in a saucepan with 50ml water and a pinch of salt. Simmer for 5 minutes to soften and warm them through.

To serve, scatter the chickpeas and red onion over the roasted squash and peppers and drizzle over the herby yoghurt.

roast vegetables with orzo and olives

Any vegetarian would be delighted with this dish. We serve this with whipped feta (page 73). Serves 4

1 red onion, sliced into thin wedges
1 head garlic, cloves separated and peeled
2 courgettes, cut into 1cm rounds
1 red romero pepper, cut into quarters and then into 3cm slices
1 aubergine, cut in quarters and then into 3cm slices
400g cherry tomatoes, whole
4 tablespoons olive oil
2 rounded teaspoons fennel seeds
1 tablespoon finely chopped rosemary
1 tablespoon thyme leaves
1 teaspoon dried oregano
100g orzo rice pasta
300ml vegetable stock
2 tablespoons black olives, stone in
juice ½ lemon
2 tablespoons roughly chopped flat-leaf parsley
whipped feta, to serve (page 73)

Preheat the oven to 220°C/425°F/gas 7.

Toss all the vegetables with the olive oil, fennel seeds and herbs, and season well with salt and pepper. Spread them out evenly on a large, high-sided roasting tray (about 25cm x 40cm) and roast in the oven for 30 minutes, until the vegetables are soft and caramelised.

Remove the tray from the oven, sprinkle over the orzo, add the stock, stir gently and season once more. Cover tightly with foil and bake for 25 minutes, then remove the foil and scatter over the olives. Return the tray to the oven for another 5 minutes.

Squeeze over the lemon juice, sprinkle over the parsley and drizzle whipped feta on top. Serve with a simple salad.

potato, cauliflower and squash with tomato and green chilli

This is a very flavourful vegetable tagine, improved with some Greek yoghurt on the side. Serves 4

2 banana shallots (120g)
3 garlic cloves
5 tablespoons olive oil
1 tablespoon ground coriander seeds
1 teaspoon ground cinnamon
1 teaspoon ground cumin seeds
1 teaspoon ground ginger
1 teaspoon ground black pepper
½ teaspoon ground turmeric
250g soft, ripe tomatoes, blitzed or finely chopped
450g cauliflower, broken into florets
200g small waxy new potatoes, e.g. Charlotte, Jersey or Ratte,
   sliced into 2cm rounds and lightly salted
250g butternut squash, peeled and cut into 2cm pieces
1 x 400g tin chickpeas, drained
500ml water
2 tablespoons chopped coriander or parsley
1 teaspoon finely chopped green chilli
200g Greek yoghurt, seasoned with ½ clove garlic crushed with
   ½ teaspoon salt

Blitz the shallots and garlic in a food processor. Heat the olive oil in a large pan over a medium heat and add the blitzed shallot and garlic, all the spices and a pinch of salt. Cook over a medium heat for 8-10 minutes, stirring occasionally, until the shallots and garlic are caramelised and soft.

Add the tomatoes, cauliflower, potatoes, squash, chickpeas and 500ml water. Bring to a simmer, then put the lid on and cook for 20 minutes, until the vegetables are tender. Check for seasoning.

Serve with the herbs and green chilli on top and the seasoned yoghurt on the side.

fish tagine with potatoes, peas and coriander

The subtle use of mixed spices and preserved lemon gives distinctive flavour to this Moroccan fish stew. Serves 4

3 tablespoons olive oil + a little extra for drizzling
2 banana shallots or 1 small red onion
2 garlic cloves
1 heaped tablespoon finely chopped preserved lemon rind (optional, page 303)
1½ heaped teaspoons ground cumin
½ teaspoon paprika
2 tablespoons finely chopped coriander + a few leaves for garnish
200g cherry tomatoes
200g small waxy new potatoes, e.g. Charlotte, Jersey or Ratte, sliced into 0.5cm rounds
200g frozen petit pois or garden peas
4 fillets of firm white fish, e.g. sea bass, monkfish or cod
slice of lemon, to serve

Using a hand blender or food processor, blitz everything except the potatoes, peas and fish. Season with salt and pepper. Transfer to a wide, deep pan with a tight-fitting lid, add the potatoes and put over a medium to high heat. Bring to a simmer, pop the lid on and cook for 5 minutes.

Add the peas and fish, replace the lid and cook for 5-8 minutes, until just cooked through. Remove from the heat, turn the fish and leave to rest for 5 minutes.

Check for seasoning and serve immediately with a drizzle of olive oil and with the extra coriander and a slice of lemon on top.

Pictured on pages 254-5

roast sea bass with fennel, potatoes and parsley and caper sauce

This recipe is for a whole fish. If you want to use fillets, roast the vegetables for 30 minutes, add the fillets and roast for another 10-15 minutes. Serves 4-6

1 large fennel bulb, cut into 3-4mm slices
500g small waxy new potatoes, e.g. Charlotte, Jersey or Ratte,
  sliced into 3mm rounds
½ small red onion, thinly sliced
1 tablespoon finely chopped rosemary
4 tablespoons olive oil
1.8kg whole sea bass for 4-6 people or 2 x 1kg bass for 4 people, gutted
  (or 4 x 160g fillets), seasoned with salt and pepper on the inside and
  outside, sprinkled with 1 teaspoon fennel seeds
100ml white wine
lemon wedges, to serve

Parsley and caper sauce
150g bunch flat-leaf parsley, stalks removed and roughly chopped
1½ tablespoons capers, rinsed thoroughly to remove the salt and squeezed dry
2 teaspoons roughly ground fennel seeds
1 small garlic clove
8 tablespoons extra virgin olive oil
juice ½ lemon

Preheat the oven to 220°C/425°F/gas 7. To make the sauce, place all the ingredients in a food processor and blitz. Check for seasoning and set aside.

In a large mixing bowl, combine the fennel, potatoes, onion, rosemary and 3 tablespoons olive oil, and season well with salt and pepper. Toss gently, then spread out evenly on a large roasting tray (about 30cm x 38cm). Put it in the over and roast for 20 minutes.

Remove from the oven and lay the sea bass diagonally across the middle of the vegetables. Pour in the wine, drizzle with the remaining olive oil and return to the oven. Roast for 30-40 minutes, or until the fish is cooked, turning the vegetables every so often so they cook evenly. For a smaller 1kg sea bass, roast the vegetables for 20 minutes, add the fish and wine then bake for 20 minutes. If using fillets, roast the vegetables for 30 minutes before adding the fillets and baking for 10 minutes.

Serve with the sauce on the side and lemon wedges.

monkfish stew with green beans, potatoes and alioli

This recipe has roots in the Ibizan *Bullit de peix*, a fish stew with flat green beans, potatoes and saffron. Sometimes the alioli, or garlic mayonnaise, (page 24) is stirred into the liquor. We prefer to serve it on the side. Serves 4

4 tablespoons olive oil
2 banana shallots, roughly chopped
2 green bell peppers, cut in half, deseeded and roughly chopped
2 garlic cloves, finely sliced
2 bay leaves
200g tomatoes, blitzed
large pinch saffron
150ml white wine
250g green (preferably flat) beans, sliced into 3cm pieces
400g potatoes, peeled, cut into small chunks and sprinkled with a little salt
500ml water
600g filleted monkfish, cut into 4–5cm pieces
2 tablespoons finely chopped flat-leaf parsley
150g alioli (page 24), or mayonnaise mixed with 1 crushed garlic clove

Heat a large saucepan over a medium heat and add the olive oil. When hot, add the shallots, green peppers, garlic and bay leaves. Add a pinch of salt, stir well and fry for 5–8 minutes, or until the shallot and peppers are soft and beginning to caramelise.

Add the blitzed tomatoes, saffron, white wine, green beans and potatoes, fry for 5 more minutes, stirring occasionally. Add the water, bring to a gentle simmer for 10 minutes, then add the monkfish and cook for another 5–6 minutes, until the fish and the potatoes are tender. Serve with the parsley on top and the alioli on the side.

whole roast turbot with garlic, rosemary and cherry tomatoes

This recipe was inspired by the Basque fish restaurants in Getaria. This dish has the wow factor – minimum effort with maximum reward. Great for a dinner party. Serves 6–8

8 tablespoons olive oil + extra for drizzling
1 x 1.5kg (for 6 people) or 2kg (for 8 people) whole turbot or brill, gutted and frills trimmed
200g cherry tomatoes, halved
2 tablespoons finely chopped rosemary
1 teaspoon fennel seeds
6 garlic cloves, sliced
2 bird's-eye chillies, crumbled
3 tablespoons good-quality apple cider vinegar (page 303) + pinch sugar
1 x 400g tin butter beans, drained
2 tablespoons finely chopped flat-leaf parsley
pinch paprika
lemon wedges, to serve

Preheat the oven to 200°C/400°F/gas 6.

Rub 2 tablespoons olive oil over the turbot and season generously with salt. Place the fish in a large roasting tin, scatter over the tomatoes, half the rosemary and the fennel seeds, drizzle with a little more olive oil, and sprinkle with salt and pepper. Place in the oven for 30–40 minutes. The turbot is cooked when the core temperature is about 55°C at its thickest part. Remove from the oven and leave to rest.

For the garlic sauce, heat the remaining olive oil over a medium heat in a medium saucepan and gently fry the garlic, chillies and remaining rosemary until the garlic is golden brown. Add the vinegar, the roast tomatoes and juices from the turbot, the butter beans and half the parsley, warm them through, then check for seasoning. Pour them over the fish and sprinkle over the remaining parsley and pinch of paprika.

Serve with lemon wedges.

baked spiced rice with tomato, prawns and green chilli

Prawn rice with spices, tomato and chilli is common in the Gulf region, and is sometimes made with dried lime. We bake this all together in the oven and serve it with yoghurt on the side. Green goddess salad (page 91), chopped salad (page 94) or courgette, lemon and basil salad without the Manchego (page 80) would all work well as a light accompaniment. Serves 4

400g sweet cherry tomatoes, halved
1 green bell pepper, deseeded and chopped into 1cm pieces
2 heads of garlic, cloves separated and peeled
½ teaspoon ground cinnamon
6 cardamom pods, cracked (optional)
1 teaspoon whole coriander seeds
4 tablespoons olive oil
500g raw shell-on prawns, peeled (keep the shells)
400ml hot vegetable stock (2 tablespoons Marigold vegetable powder
    mixed with boiling water)
200g basmati rice
4 tablespoons chopped coriander
4 teaspoons chopped green chilli
200g Greek yoghurt, mixed with ½ garlic clove, crushed with salt,
    and ½ teaspoon baharat or allspice
lemon or lime wedges, to serve

Preheat the oven to 180°C/350°F/gas 4.

Toss the tomatoes, green pepper and garlic with the spices, olive oil, salt and pepper and spread out on a large roasting tray (30–40cm). Roast in the oven for 35–40 minutes, until soft.

Meanwhile add the prawn shells to the vegetable stock (you can just use water) and simmer gently for 15 minutes to flavour the stock. Strain to remove the shells, then season the stock to taste.

Sprinkle the rice over the vegetables, then add the hot stock and mix evenly. Cover tightly with foil and bake in the oven at 200°C/400°F/gas 6 for 20 minutes. Remove the foil and add the prawns, tucking them into the rice, then return it to the oven for another 2–4 minutes, until the prawns and rice are cooked (2 minutes for smaller Atlantic prawns, 4 minutes for larger tiger prawns).

Fluff up the rice with a fork, and serve with the coriander and fresh green chilli on top, and the yoghurt and lemon or lime wedges on the side.

roast chicken, wild rice, mushrooms and sweet herbs

The addition of turmeric brightens the overall look of this recipe. Serves 4

2 tablespoons olive oil
25g butter
2 leeks (white part only), cut in half lengthways and thinly sliced
2 bay leaves
400g mixed mushrooms (field, wild and oyster), sliced
200g mixed wild and basmati rice
400ml vegetable or chicken stock
4 organic chicken breasts, skin removed and seasoned with salt and pepper
200g Greek yoghurt, seasoned with ½ garlic clove crushed with salt
    and 1 level teaspoon turmeric
3 tablespoons each chopped tarragon, dill, parsley and basil
½ teaspoon Aleppo chilli flakes (page 304)

Preheat the oven to 200°C/400°F/gas 6.

Place a large (about 30cm) heavy ovenproof casserole pan with a tight-fitting lid over a medium heat and add the oil and butter. When the butter begins to foam, add the leeks and bay leaves and a good pinch of salt, and fry for 10 minutes or until the leeks are soft and sweet, stirring occasionally.

Add the mushrooms and continue to cook, stirring occasionally, until the mushrooms are soft and the liquid they have released has almost evaporated (about 5 minutes). Stir in the rice and the stock and bring to a gentle simmer.

Lay the chicken on top, season with salt and pepper and cover with the lid. Place in the oven for 20 minutes, then remove the lid and continue cooking for another 5–10 minutes, until the rice is cooked, the chicken is cooked through (juices run clear).

Remove from the oven and lift out the chicken to rest for a couple of minutes. Stir the yoghurt mixture and two-thirds of the sweet herbs into the rice. Slice the chicken and serve with the rest of the herbs on top and sprinkled with chilli flakes.

lamb with spring vegetables

We highly recommend making this dish when spring vegetables start to appear, as it is a celebration of the new season! Serves 4

2 tablespoons olive oil
600g boneless lamb shoulder, trimmed, cut into 2cm cubes
2 tablespoons fresh thyme leaves
1 heaped tablespoon flour or cornflour
100ml white wine
300ml water
800ml full-fat milk
150g new potatoes or small waxy ones, cut into 5mm slices
280g jar artichoke hearts, drained (200g) and cut in quarters
10 asparagus spears, trimmed and sliced into 3cm lengths
250g petits pois or garden peas, frozen
3 tablespoons chopped mint leaves

Place a large saucepan over a medium heat and add the olive oil. When the oil is hot, add the lamb, thyme and 2 teaspoons salt and cook for 5 minutes. Remove the lid, stir in the flour, making sure it is mixed thoroughly, then add the white wine, 300ml water and stir well. Simmer the lamb for 10 minutes, then add the milk and continue to simmer for a further 15 minutes.

Add the potatoes and cook until just tender, about 10 minutes. Add the artichokes, asparagus, peas and half the mint and cook for another 10 minutes, until the lamb is tender.

Stir in the remaining mint, rest for 5 minutes, then serve.

tomato bulgur with lamb and cinnamon yoghurt

Chopped salad (page 94) is a fitting side instead of green salad. Serves 4

2 tablespoons olive oil
50g butter
1 large leek, finely chopped
2 garlic cloves, finely sliced
1 green bell pepper, deseeded and finely chopped
1 large aubergine, cut into 2cm cubes and lightly salted
400g lamb shoulder, cut into 2cm cubes
300g tomato passata
1 teaspoon ground cinnamon
800ml of water
250g medium or coarse bulgur, washed well and drained
200g Greek yoghurt, mixed with ½ teaspoon ground cinnamon
4 tablespoons chopped coriander or parsley
1 tablespoon finely chopped green chilli

Put the oil and butter into a medium (25cm) saucepan over a medium heat. When the butter begins to foam, add the leek, garlic, green pepper, aubergine and a pinch of salt and fry for 10-15 minutes, stirring occasionally, until soft and sweet. Take off the heat and rest for a few minutes, then transfer to a bowl and set aside.

Using the same pan, add the lamb, passata, cinnamon and cover with 800ml of water. Simmer with the lid on for about 1 hour, until the lamb is tender. Season with salt and pepper, then stir in the bulgur and the vegetables. Simmer with the lid on for another 5 minutes, until the bulgur has absorbed all the liquid.

Rest for 5 minutes with the lid on, then serve with the cinnamon yoghurt on the side and the coriander or parsley and chilli sprinkled on top.

lamb tagine with carrots and potatoes

This is one of our favourite slow-cooked lamb dishes; with some subtle spices the humble meat and two veg is transformed into something exotic and special. Serves 4

5 tablespoons olive oil
1 teaspoon each ground ginger, cinnamon, cumin and black pepper
½ teaspoon ground turmeric
4 banana shallots, blitzed to a purée
4 tablespoons chopped coriander + extra for garnish
800g boneless lamb shoulder, trimmed of fat and cut into 3cm cubes
approx. 1 litre water
450g carrots, peeled and cut into 4cm chunks
500g potatoes, peeled and cut into 4cm chunks

Place a large (25cm) saucepan over a medium heat and add the olive oil, spices, blitzed shallots and a pinch of salt. Cook for 10 minutes, until the shallots begin to caramelise, then add the coriander and lamb and sauté for 10 more minutes, stirring occasionally.

Add enough water to almost cover the lamb and simmer, lid on, for 30 minutes. Add the carrots and potatoes, season well with salt, and cook for 40–45 more minutes until everything is tender.

Let the tagine rest for 5 minutes, then serve with the extra coriander sprinkled on top.

easy desserts

These desserts satisfy that need for 'a little something sweet' at the end of a meal. The ice creams require no churning, the cakes are quick to bake, and the ingredients minimal.

pistachio madeleines

Madeleines are always best served straight out of the oven. Make the batter, then bake the madeleines 10-15 minutes before you want to serve them. They are an excellent accompaniment to the ice creams (pages 282 and 283). Makes 24

100g butter (room temperature) + extra for greasing
100g caster sugar
2 free-range or organic eggs, lightly beaten
finely grated zest 1 lemon + extra for serving
70g very finely ground pistachios + extra for serving
50g self-raising flour, sieved + extra for dusting

Beat the butter and sugar until very pale and light, approximately 10 minutes. Stir in the eggs one by one, ensuring the first is fully incorporated before adding the second, followed by the lemon zest and pistachios. Once combined, gently fold in the flour. Leave the batter to rest in the fridge overnight.

Preheat the oven to 190°C/375°F/gas 5.

Generously grease two madeleine or cupcake trays with butter and lightly dust with flour, tapping off any excess.

Spoon a dessertspoon of the mixture into each mould, being careful not to overfill them – this quantity should make 24 madeleines. Bake for 10-12 minutes, until golden.

Serve with the extra pistachios and lemon zest sprinkled over.

chocolate almond cake

My friend Sara Fanelli baked this gluten-free cake for us. We love it especially with a little sea salt on top. Makes 8–10 slices

175g dark chocolate, broken into chunks
175g unsalted butter + extra for greasing
175g caster sugar
175g ground almonds
4 free-range or organic eggs, separated
sea salt

Preheat the oven to 160°C/325°F/gas 3.

Generously grease a 23cm cake tin with butter and line the base with baking paper.

Put the chunks of chocolate into a bain-marie (a heatproof bowl set over barely simmering water). Once melted, remove from the heat and stir in the butter to melt. Stir in the caster sugar, ground almonds and a small pinch of sea salt. Set aside to cool slightly. Meanwhile, whisk the egg whites to soft, fluffy peaks.

Once the chocolate mixture has cooled slightly, stir in the egg yolks. Using a metal spoon, stir in one heaped spoonful of the whisked egg whites. Once this spoonful is fully incorporated, gently fold in the remaining egg whites.

Gently pour the batter into the prepared cake tin and lightly sprinkle the top with flaky sea salt. Bake for 40–45 minutes, until the top is crackled and the cake feels slightly springy to the touch.

Allow to cool in the tin before removing and placing on a wire rack. Cut into slices to serve.

coffee, walnut and cardamom muffins

The date molasses finishes off these muffins perfectly. Makes 12 muffins

Muffins
175g butter (room temperature)
175g caster sugar
3 free-range or organic eggs
150g self-raising flour, sieved
70g walnuts, chopped into small pieces
1 tablespoon instant coffee powder
8 cardamom pods, seeds finely ground

Icing
50g butter (room temperature)
50g icing sugar, sieved
1 tablespoon instant coffee powder, slackened with ½ tablespoon
   just-boiled water
100g cream cheese

To serve
date molasses, for drizzling (optional)

Preheat the oven to 160°C/325°F/gas 3 and line a muffin tray with cases.

For the muffins, cream the butter and sugar until very pale and fluffy, approximately 10 minutes. Add the eggs one by one, ensuring each one has been incorporated before adding the next. Fold in the flour, walnuts, coffee and cardamom. Spoon into the muffin cases and bake for 25–30 minutes, until golden and a skewer comes out clean when inserted. Remove from the tin to cool on a wire rack.

For the icing, cream the butter and icing sugar until very pale, at least 5 minutes. Add the coffee and continue to beat until completely incorporated. Finally, stir in the cream cheese.

Once the muffins are completely cool, top with the icing, then drizzle with date molasses, if you like, just before serving.

coffee and cardamom ice cream

The flavours of Turkish coffee also work so well as an ice cream.
Makes one large tub (approx. 800ml). Serves around 8

2 tablespoons instant espresso powder
12 cardamom pods, seeds finely ground
175g condensed milk
300ml double cream

Whisk all the ingredients together into soft peaks. Transfer to a container and freeze.

Pictured on page 285

mint chocolate ice cream

Mint choc without the chip. Makes one large tub (approx. 600ml).
Serves 6-8

300ml double cream
40 mint leaves
200g dark chocolate, broken into chunks
175g condensed milk

Put the cream and mint leaves into a medium saucepan and just bring to a simmer. Pour the mixture into a heatproof bowl, allow to cool, then cover and refrigerate for at least 2 hours (or longer, if you have time) to infuse.

Pass the cream mixture through a fine sieve, squeezing the mint leaves to maximise their flavour.

Melt the chocolate in a bain-marie (a heatproof bowl set over barely simmering water), then set aside to cool slightly.

Whisk the cold infused cream with the condensed milk for 5 minutes to thicken (it won't whip into peaks). Fold in the melted chocolate, transfer to a container and freeze.

Pictured on page 285

raspberry and yoghurt fool

The genius of this recipe is the use of frozen raspberries. Makes one large tub (approx. 600ml). Serves 6–8

350g frozen raspberries
250g Greek yoghurt
3 tablespoons runny honey

Chill four glasses or small bowls in advance of dishing up.

Just before you are ready to serve, blitz all the ingredients in a food processor until just smooth and thick, being careful not to over-process.

Scoop into the chilled glasses or bowls and serve immediately.

Pictured on page 285

sea salt almond brittle ice cream

My favourite Baskin-Robbins ice cream from the 1970s was English Toffee. We have tried to replicate the flavours here by making an almond brittle and stirring it through the ice cream. Makes one large tub (approx. 800ml). Serves around 8

Brittle
100g caster sugar
1 tablespoon butter
50g roasted almonds

Ice cream
300ml double cream
175g condensed milk
1 vanilla pod, cut in half lengthways and seeds scraped out

Line a baking tray with baking paper.

Place a heavy saucepan over a medium heat. Add the sugar and swirl the pan to gently melt it. Continue to cook until the melted sugar becomes a dark caramel (the exact time will depend on your pan, so keep a constant eye on it, swirling the pan every so often to ensure that the sugar is cooking evenly), then add the butter, roasted almonds and a good pinch of sea salt. Briefly stir to combine, then quickly pour the caramel onto the lined tray and leave to cool.

Once cool, carefully chop the brittle into small pieces.

Whisk the cream, condensed milk and vanilla seeds to soft peaks. Fold in the brittle pieces, then transfer to a container and freeze.

Pictured on page 285

rosewater rice pudding with rhubarb and cardamom compote

Rice pudding gently perfumed with rosewater is wonderful and perfect with the sharpness of the rhubarb compote. Serves 4-6

Rice pudding
butter, for greasing
100g pudding rice
70g caster sugar
2 teaspoons rosewater
zest 1 lemon
1 litre whole milk
2 tablespoons finely ground pistachios

Rhubarb and cardamom compote
400g rhubarb, trimmed and cut into 2-3cm chunks, depending on thickness
100g caster sugar
5 cardamom pods, seeds finely ground
50ml water

Preheat the oven to 150°C/300°F/gas 2 and generously grease a 25cm round baking dish with butter.

Mix all the rice pudding ingredients together and pour into the greased baking dish. Bake for 1 hour 45 minutes to 2 hours, until a skin has formed on top and the rice is tender.

While the rice pudding bakes, put all the compote ingredients into a medium saucepan and cook over a medium heat for 12-15 minutes, until the rhubarb is soft. Remove from the heat and set aside to cool.

Serve the compote with the rice pudding. Delicious warm or cold.

MARIA SANTISIMA
DE LA CONCEPCIÓN

lemon crème brûlée

Rich, lemony with a thin crunch from the brûlée. Makes 8

600ml double cream
3 lemons, zest peeled + 1 cut into eighths, to serve
1 vanilla pod, cut in half lengthways and seeds scraped out
7 free-range or organic egg yolks
140g golden caster sugar
2 tablespoons lemon juice

Preheat the oven to 150°C/300°F/gas 2.

In a saucepan, heat the cream with the lemon zest, vanilla pod and seeds
over a low heat. Bring to a simmer (be careful it doesn't boil), then take off
the heat and pass through a fine sieve.

Whisk the yolks and 100g sugar until pale and fluffy. Still whisking, add
a third of the cream mixture until you get a smooth mix. Add the rest of the
cream and the lemon juice, stirring constantly.

Pour the mixture into eight ramekins. Place them in a deep baking tray
and add boiling water to the tray until it is halfway up the sides of the
ramekins. Bake for 25–30 minutes. The custards should be firm but retains
a bit of movement. Allow to cool, then refrigerate for at least 4 hours,
preferably overnight.

To serve, top with the rest of the sugar (5g for each ramekin), then
flash under a very hot grill – or use a blowtorch – until the sugar melts
and caramelises, giving you a crunchy crust. Serve each one with a
lemon wedge.

lemon and mint *granizado*

Fresh mint lemonade is a favourite drink (sherbet) in Syria; here we have made those flavours into a *granizado* (Spanish for granita). Serves around 8

10 lemons
1 litre water
150g sugar
15 tablespoons whole mint leaves

Zest 4 lemons and set the zest aside, then juice the lemons until you have 150ml of liquid.

Place the water, zest and sugar in a saucepan and bring to a gentle simmer for a couple of minutes. Remove from the heat, add the lemon juice and leave to cool.

In a food processor, blend the mint leaves with 200ml of the now-cool liquid. Return the puréed mint to the pan. Strain the liquid into a 2-litre container (squeeze the mint dry) and leave overnight in the freezer.

To serve, scrape the surface with a fork or spoon to lift off the shavings of this refreshing *granizado*.

yoghurt cheesecake with muscatel strawberries

Our brilliant recipe tester Florence Blair suggested pairing this cheesecake with lemon thyme. It works really well. Makes 8–10 slices

Base
200g digestive biscuits
50g butter, melted

Filling
500g strained Greek yoghurt
400g cream cheese
120g icing sugar, sieved
zest 1 lemon

Muscatel strawberries
400g strawberries, halved
squeeze lemon
1 tablespoon caster sugar
100ml muscatel + 1 tablespoon extra for serving
2 teaspoons lemon thyme leaves for serving

Line the base and sides of a 23cm springform or loose-bottomed round tin with baking paper.

For the base, blitz the digestive biscuits to a fine powder. Combine the biscuits with the melted butter and spoon into the lined tin, pressing down to form an even layer. Put into the fridge to set while you make the filling.

Beat the yoghurt and cream cheese together. Stir in the sieved icing sugar and the lemon zest. Spoon this mixture over the biscuit base and smooth out the top. Transfer it to the fridge and leave to set overnight.

Put all the ingredients for the muscatel strawberries, except the extra tablespoon of muscatel, into a medium saucepan and cook over a gentle heat for 8–10 minutes, until the fruit has softened.

Allow to cool to room temperature, then stir through the final tablespoon of muscatel before serving.

Serve the cheesecake with the muscatel strawberries and lemon thyme sprinkled on top.

suppliers

Below are a handful of suppliers for some of the specialist store cupboard ingredients that are of excellent quality. We particularly recommend the vinegars as they do make a difference to the overall flavour.

MIDDLE EASTERN STORE CUPBOARD

BELAZU www.belazu.com
We are very proud of our ex-head chef at Moro, Henry Russell, who heads up the development kitchen at Belazu.
extra virgin olive oil
moscatel vinegar
cabernet sauvignon or merlot red wine vinegar
vermouth wine vinegar
chardonnay white wine vinegar
white balsamic vinegar
sherry vinegar
apple cider vinegar
tahini (good quality)
pomegranate molasses
date molasses
beldi preserved lemons
pickled Zahter (to use instead of dry za'atar)
olives (a wonderful selection)

SPANISH STORE CUPBOARD

MEVALCO www.mevalco.com
extra virgin olive oil
cabernet sauvignon red wine vinegar
sherry vinegar
moscatel vinegar
chardonnay white wine vinegar
smoked mild (dulce) and hot paprika
sweet smoked pepper flakes
ibérico and serrano ham
chorizo picante
Manchego cheese
Valencia fried salted almonds
piquillo peppers
salted anchovies

Continued on page 304

BRINDISA www.brindisa.com
piquillo peppers
pickled green chillies
ibérico and serrano ham
chorizo (cooking)
Ortiz anchovies
smoked sweet and hot paprika
saffron
sherry
Albariño wine
Manchego and Picos blue cheeses
cabernet sauvignon red wine vinegar
moscatel vinegar
sherry vinegar

ROOTED SPICES www.rootedspices.com
allspice
za'atar
Turkish/Aleppo chilli flakes (pul biber)
sumac
cinnamon (ground)
coriander (whole and ground)
cumin (whole and ground)
fennel seeds
nigella seeds
cardamom
ginger
turmeric
za'atar blend

MISC
stock – Marigold vegetable stock

index

A

Albariño wine, scallops with **198**

alioli: crab, Oloroso sherry and alioli toast **30**

    monkfish stew with green beans, potatoes and alioli **259**

    tortilla, green pepper and alioli toast **24-5**

almonds: ceviche with green apple and almond sauce **178**

    chocolate almond cake **279**

    kale, preserved lemon and toasted almonds salad **79**

    sea salt almond brittle ice cream **287**

anchovies: anchovy, rosemary and paprika butter lamb chops **240-1**

    pepper, anchovy and chopped egg toast **18**

    tomato, avocado and anchovy toast **21**

    turbot with anchovy, rosemary and paprika butter **204**

apples: autumn salad **85**

    beetroot, apple and mint salad **95**

    ceviche with green apple and almond sauce **178**

artichokes: artichoke salsa with olives, capers and sun-dried tomatoes **102**

    boiled artichokes with za'atar **105**

asparagus: asparagus, orange butter sauce and toasted hazelnuts **123**

    clams, white wine and asparagus **197**

    labneh, asparagus, chilli butter and dukkah **54**

    lentils, peas, asparagus and broad beans **158**

    scallops, roast asparagus and thyme dressing **201**

aubergines: roasted aubergines, pomegranates and pistachios **111**

    roasted aubergines, tomatoes and tahini **108**

autumn salad **85**

avocados: ceviche with pomegranate, lime and avocado **177**

    green goddess salad **91**

    tomato, avocado and anchovy toast **21**

B

baharat: chicken livers, baharat and pomegranate molasses **219**

barley: oyster mushroom broth with barley and sweet herbs **157**

beef: seared beef with blue cheese sauce and roast mushrooms **236**

    steak, red wine and onion toast **35**

beetroot: beetroot, apple and mint salad **95**

    roast red onions and beetroot with pomegranates **134**

bread: chorizo, tomato and chilli toast **21**

    courgette, mint and jamón toast **26**

    crab, Oloroso sherry and alioli toast **30**

    easy flatbread **144**

    goat's cheese and roasted red onion toast **32**

    pepper, anchovy and chopped egg toast **18**

    pork, green pepper and jamón toast **33**

    steak, red wine and onion toast **35**

    tomato and jamón toast **22**

    tomato, avocado and anchovy toast **21**

    tortilla, green pepper and alioli toast **24-5**

brittle: sea salt almond brittle ice cream **287**

broad beans, lentils, peas, asparagus and **158**

broth: oyster mushroom broth with barley and sweet herbs **157**

brown shrimps and spiced brown butter **168**

bulgur: leek, pepper and walnut bulgur pilaf **153**

tomato bulgur with lamb and cinnamon yoghurt **271**

butter: anchovy, rosemary and paprika butter **204**

asparagus, orange butter sauce and toasted hazelnuts **123**

brown shrimps and spiced brown butter **168**

chilli butter **150**

C

cabbage: red cabbage, caraway and red chilli salad **88**

cacık, fried courgettes with **114**

cakes: chocolate almond cake **279**

coffee, walnut and cardamom muffins **281**

pistachio madeleines **276**

capers: artichoke salsa with olives, capers and sun-dried tomatoes **102**

roast sea bass with fennel, potatoes and parsley and caper sauce **256**

squid and tomato salad with crispy capers **181**

caraway seeds: labneh, carrots, caraway and pistachios **70**

red cabbage, caraway and red chilli salad **88**

cardamom: coffee and cardamom ice cream **282**

coffee, walnut and cardamom muffins **281**

rosewater rice pudding with rhubarb and cardamom compote **288**

carrots: labneh, carrots, caraway and pistachios **70**

lamb tagine with carrots and potatoes **272**

cashews: dukkah **54**

cauliflower: potato, cauliflower and squash with tomato and green chilli **252**

ceviches: ceviche with citrus salad and pistachios **170**

ceviche with courgettes, lemon and basil **175**

ceviche with green apple and almond sauce **178**

ceviche with pomegranate, lime and avocado **177**

cheese: courgette, lemon, basil and Manchego cheese salad **80**

fried halloumi, honey and sesame **74**

fried potatoes with za'atar, peppers and feta **137**

goat's cheese and roasted red onion toast **32**

marinated feta, cherry tomatoes and olives **72**

omelette with sweet herbs, feta, pine nuts and sumac **50**

roast vegetables with orzo and olives **250**

seared beef with blue cheese sauce and roast mushrooms **236**

seared mushrooms with Manchego **127**

Turkish eggs with spinach, tomato, feta and dill **48**

watermelon, cos and feta salad **92**

whipped feta **73**

cheesecake: yoghurt cheesecake with muscatel strawberries **298**

chicken: chicken salad with orange, grapefruit, mint and pistachio sauce **220**

chicken with preserved lemon labneh **223**

roast chicken, wild rice, mushrooms and sweet herbs **265**

roast chicken with two marinades **222**

chicken livers: chicken liver pâté with Oloroso sherry **216**

chicken livers, baharat and pomegranate molasses **219**

chickpeas: mussels with yoghurt, dill and crispy chickpeas **190**

roast squash, peppers, chickpeas and herby yoghurt **249**

spinach and chickpeas **162**

chicory: autumn salad **85**

green goddess salad **91**

chilli butter **150**

fried eggs with yoghurt and chilli butter **38**

labneh, asparagus, chilli butter and dukkah **54**

labneh, mushrooms, sweet herbs and chilli butter **67**

chillies: baked spiced rice with tomato, prawns and green chilli **263**

chilli butter **150**

chorizo, tomato and chilli toast **21**

eggs with chorizo, tomato and green chilli **41**

potato, cauliflower and squash with tomato and green chilli **252**

red cabbage, caraway and red chilli salad **88**

shakshuka with green chilli and coriander salsa **44-7**

squid kofte with mojo verde **184**

tuna with fennel seeds, oregano and chilli **212**

chocolate: chocolate almond cake **279**

mint chocolate ice cream **283**

chopped salad **94**

chorizo: chorizo, tomato and chilli toast **21**

eggs with chorizo, tomato and green chilli **41**

fried eggs, peas and chorizo **43**

lentils and chorizo **165**

spring greens with crispy chorizo **124**

citrus fruit: ceviche with citrus salad and pistachios **170** clams: clams, white wine and asparagus **197**

clams, white wine and coriander **194**

coffee: coffee and cardamom ice cream **282**

coffee, walnut and cardamom muffins **281**

compote, rhubarb and cardamom **288**

courgettes: ceviche with courgettes, lemon and basil **175**

courgette, lemon, basil and Manchego cheese salad **80**

courgette, mint and jamón toast **26**

fried courgettes with cacık **114**

labneh, courgette, tomato and mint **64**

crab, Oloroso sherry and alioli toast **30**

cream: coffee and cardamom ice cream **282**

lemon crème brûlée **292**

mint chocolate ice cream **283**

sea salt almond brittle ice cream **287**

cream cheese: yoghurt cheesecake with muscatel strawberries **298**

crème brûlée, lemon **292**

cucumber: cacık **114**

chopped salad **94**

cucumber, tahini sauce and chilli salad **83**

labneh, tomato, cucumber and za'atar **61**

D

dip: cacık **114**

duck breasts with walnut and pomegranate sauce **226**

dukkah: labneh, asparagus, chilli butter and dukkah **54**

spiced labneh, tomatoes, mint and dukkah **68**

E

eggs: eggs with chorizo, tomato and green chilli **41**

fried eggs, peas and chorizo **43**

fried eggs with toasted cumin **38**

fried eggs with yoghurt and chilli butter **38**

lemon crème brûlée **292**

omelette with sweet herbs, feta, pine nuts and sumac **50**

pepper, anchovy and chopped egg toast **18**

shakshuka with green chilli and coriander salsa **44-7**

Turkish eggs with spinach, tomato, feta and dill **48**

erişte with leeks, yoghurt and walnuts **160**

F

fennel: labneh, sun-dried tomato, coriander and fennel seeds **57**

roast sea bass with fennel, potatoes and parsley and caper sauce **256**

fennel seeds: roast chicken with fennel seed, garlic and thyme marinade **222**

tuna with fennel seeds, oregano and chilli **212**

fenugreek: roast chicken with fenugreek and coriander marinade **222**

fig leaves: sea bass baked with fig leaves and walnut sauce **205**

figs: autumn salad **85**

fish **166-213**

anchovy, rosemary and paprika butter lamb chops **240-1**

ceviche with citrus salad and pistachios **170**

ceviche with courgettes, lemon and basil **175**

ceviche with green apple and almond sauce **178**

ceviche with pomegranate, lime and avocado **177**

fish tagine with potatoes, peas and coriander **253**

fried monkfish with lemon, garlic, coriander and dill **208**

mackerel with tomato, olive and sherry vinaigrette **210**

monkfish stew with green beans, potatoes and alioli **259**

pepper, anchovy and chopped egg toast **18**

roast sea bass with fennel, potatoes and parsley and caper sauce **256**

sea bass baked with fig leaves and walnut sauce **205**

sea bass with migas, lemon zest, garlic and parsley **203**

tomato, avocado and anchovy toast **21**

tuna with fennel seeds, oregano and chilli **212**

turbot with anchovy, rosemary and paprika butter **204**

whole roast turbot with garlic, rosemary and cherry tomatoes **261**

flatbread, easy **144**

fool, raspberry and yoghurt **286**

ful medames **142**

G

garlic: roast squash, sweet vinegar, garlic and rosemary **118**

sea bass with migas, lemon zest, garlic and parsley **203**

whole roast turbot with garlic, rosemary and cherry tomatoes **261**

granizado, lemon and mint **297**

grapefruit: chicken salad with orange, grapefruit, mint and pistachio sauce **220**

grapes: autumn salad **85**

green beans: monkfish stew with green beans, potatoes and alioli **259**

green goddess salad **91**

H

halloumi: fried halloumi, honey and sesame **74**

hazelnuts, asparagus, orange butter sauce and toasted **123**

herbs: herby yoghurt **249**

    labneh, mushrooms, sweet herbs and chilli butter **67**

    omelette with sweet herbs, feta, pine nuts and sumac **50**

    oyster mushroom broth with barley and sweet herbs **157**

    roast chicken, wild rice, mushrooms and sweet herbs **265**

honey: fried halloumi, honey and sesame **74**

I

ice cream: coffee and cardamom ice cream **282**

    mint chocolate ice cream **283**

    sea salt almond brittle ice cream **287**

J

jamón: courgette, mint and jamón toast **26**

    peas with jamón and mint **139**

    pork, green pepper and jamón toast **33**

    tomato and jamón toast **22**

    veal escalopes, rosemary and jamón **233**

K

kale: kale, preserved lemon and toasted almonds salad **79**

    kale purée with polenta **128**

kofte: squid kofte with *mojo verde* **184**

L

labneh: chicken with preserved lemon labneh **223**

    labneh, asparagus, chilli butter and dukkah **54**

labneh, carrots, caraway and pistachios **70**

labneh, courgette, tomato and mint **64**

labneh, mushrooms, sweet herbs and chilli butter **67**

labneh, sun-dried tomato, coriander and fennel seeds **57**

labneh, sweetcorn, coriander and paprika **58**

labneh, tomato, cucumber and za'atar **61**

spiced labneh, tomatoes, mint and dukkah **68**

lamb: lamb chops three ways **240–1**

    lamb tagine with carrots and potatoes **272**

    lamb with spring vegetables **268**

    Maghrebi slow-roast shoulder of lamb **245**

    tomato bulgur with lamb and cinnamon yoghurt **271**

leeks: erişte with leeks, yoghurt and walnuts **160**

    leek, pepper and walnut bulgur pilaf **153**

lemons: ceviche with courgettes, lemon and basil **175**

    courgette, lemon, basil and Manchego cheese salad **80**

    fried monkfish with lemon, garlic, coriander and dill **208**

    lemon and mint granizado **297**

    lemon crème brûlée **292**

    sea bass with migas, lemon zest, garlic and parsley **203**

lemons, preserved: chicken with preserved lemon labneh **223**

    kale, preserved lemon and toasted almonds salad **79**

lentils: lentils and chorizo **165**

    lentils, peas, asparagus and broad beans **158**

    red lentil, pepper and walnut salad with tarragon **98-9**

    red lentil soup with yoghurt and mint **150**

lettuce: autumn salad **85**

    gem lettuce, peas and pancetta **117**

    green goddess salad **91**

    watermelon, cos and feta salad **92**

lime: ceviche with pomegranate, lime and avocado **177**

M

mackerel with tomato, olive and sherry vinaigrette **210**

madeleines, pistachio **276**

Maghrebi slow-roast shoulder of lamb **245**

menemen **48**

migas: sea bass with migas, lemon zest, garlic and parsley **203**

mint: hot mint sauce **241**

    mint chocolate ice cream **283**

mojo verde, squid kofte with **184**

monkfish stew with green beans, potatoes and alioli **259**

muffins, coffee, walnut and cardamom **281**

muscatel strawberries, yoghurt cheesecake with **298**

mushrooms: labneh, mushrooms, sweet herbs and chilli butter **67**

    oyster mushroom broth with barley and sweet herbs **157**

    roast chicken, wild rice, mushrooms and sweet herbs **265**

    seared beef with blue cheese sauce and roast mushrooms **236**

    seared mushrooms with Manchego **127**

mussels: mussel and potato salad with paprika dressing **187**

    mussels with yoghurt, dill and crispy chickpeas **190**

O

olives: artichoke salsa with olives, capers and sun-dried tomatoes **102** mackerel with tomato, olive and sherry vinaigrette 210

marinated feta, cherry tomatoes and olives 72

roast vegetables with orzo and olives 250

Oloroso sherry: chicken liver pâté with Oloroso sherry 216

crab, Oloroso sherry and alioli toast 30

omelette with sweet herbs, feta, pine nuts and sumac 50

onions: goat's cheese and roasted red onion toast 32

roast red onions and beetroot with pomegranates 134

steak, red wine and onion toast 35

orange juice: asparagus, orange butter sauce and toasted hazelnuts 123

roast shoulder of pork marinated with orange and cumin 238

oranges: chicken salad with orange, grapefruit, mint and pistachio sauce 220

orzo: roast vegetables with orzo and olives 250

P

pancetta, gem lettuce, peas and 117

pasta: erişte with leeks, yoghurt and walnuts 160

roast vegetables with orzo and olives 250

pâté, chicken liver 216

peas: fish tagine with potatoes, peas and coriander 253

fried eggs, peas and chorizo 43

gem lettuce, peas and pancetta 117

lentils, peas, asparagus and broad beans 158

peas with jamón and mint 139

peppers: fried potatoes with za'atar, peppers and feta 137

leek, pepper and walnut bulgur pilaf 153

pepper, anchovy and chopped egg toast 18

pork, green pepper and jamón toast 33

pork fillet with roast peppers 228

red lentil, pepper and walnut salad with tarragon 98-9

roast squash, peppers, chickpeas and herby yoghurt 249

tortilla, green pepper and alioli toast 24-5

pilaf: brown rice and potato pilaf 149

leek, pepper and walnut bulgur pilaf 153

pine nuts: omelette with sweet herbs, feta, pine nuts and sumac 50

spinach, pine nuts and sultanas 133

pistachios: ceviche with citrus salad and pistachios 170

chicken salad with orange, grapefruit, mint and pistachio sauce 220

labneh, carrots, caraway and pistachios 70

pistachio madeleines 276

roasted aubergines, pomegranates and pistachios 111

polenta, kale purée with 128

pomegranate molasses, chicken livers, baharat and 219

pomegranates: autumn salad 85

ceviche with pomegranate, lime and avocado 177

duck breasts with walnut and pomegranate sauce 226

roasted aubergines, pomegranates and pistachios 111

roast red onions and beetroot with pomegranates 134

pork: pork, green pepper and jamón toast 33

pork fillet with roast peppers 228

roast shoulder of pork marinated with orange and cumin 238

potatoes: brown rice and potato pilaf 149

fish tagine with potatoes, peas and coriander 253

fried potatoes with za'atar, peppers and feta 137

lamb tagine with carrots and potatoes 272

monkfish stew with green beans, potatoes and alioli 259

mussel and potato salad with paprika dressing 187

potato, cauliflower and squash with tomato and green chilli 252

roast sea bass with fennel, potatoes and parsley and caper sauce 256

spiced potato cake 104

squid, potatoes, red wine and rosemary 182

tortilla, green pepper and alioli toast 24-5

prawns: baked spiced rice with tomato, prawns and green chilli 263

prego toast 35

R

raspberry and yoghurt fool 286

red wine: squid, potatoes, red wine and rosemary 182

steak, red wine and onion toast 35

rhubarb: rosewater rice pudding with rhubarb and cardamom compote 288

rice: baked spiced rice with tomato, prawns and green chilli 263

brown rice and potato pilaf 149

roast chicken, wild rice, mushrooms and sweet herbs 265

rosewater rice pudding with rhubarb and cardamom compote 288

S

salads 76-99

autumn salad 85

beetroot, apple and mint salad 95

ceviche with citrus salad and pistachios 170

chicken salad with orange, grapefruit, mint and pistachio sauce 220

chopped salad 94

courgette, lemon, basil and Manchego cheese salad 80

cucumber, tahini sauce and chilli salad 83

green goddess salad 91

kale, preserved lemon and toasted almond salad 79

mussel and potato salad with paprika dressing 187

red cabbage, caraway and red chilli salad 88

red lentil, pepper and walnut salad with tarragon 98-9

squid and tomato salad with crispy capers 181

watermelon, cos and feta salad 92

salsas: artichoke salsa with olives, capers and sun-dried tomatoes 102

green chilli and coriander salsa 44-7

scallops: scallops, roast asparagus and thyme dressing 201

scallops with Albariño wine 198

sea bass: roast sea bass with fennel, potatoes and parsley and caper sauce 256

sea bass with migas, lemon zest, garlic and parsley 203

sea salt almond brittle ice cream 287

serranito toast 33

sesame seeds: dukkah 54

fried halloumi, honey and sesame 74

shakshuka with green chilli and coriander salsa 44-7

sherry: chicken liver pâté with Oloroso sherry 216

crab, Oloroso sherry and alioli toast 30

shrimps: brown shrimps and spiced brown butter 168

soup, red lentil 150

spiced labneh, tomatoes, mint and dukkah 68

spiced potato cake 104

spinach: spinach and chickpeas 162

spinach, pine nuts and sultanas 133

Turkish eggs with spinach, tomato, feta and dill 48

spring greens with crispy chorizo 124

squash: potato, cauliflower and squash with tomato and green chilli 252

roast squash, peppers, chickpeas and herby yoghurt 249

roast squash, sweet vinegar, garlic and rosemary 118

squid: squid and tomato salad with crispy capers 181

squid, potatoes, red wine and rosemary 182

squid kofte with mojo verde 184

steak, red wine and onion toast 35

stew: monkfish stew with green beans, potatoes and alioli 259

strawberries, yoghurt cheesecake with muscatel 298

sultanas, spinach, pine nuts and 133

sumac, omelette with sweet herbs, feta, pine nuts and 50

sweetcorn: labneh, sweetcorn, coriander and paprika 58

T

tagines: fish tagine with potatoes, peas and coriander 253

lamb tagine with carrots and potatoes 272

tahini: cucumber, tahini sauce and chilli salad 83

roasted aubergines, tomatoes and tahini 108

toasts, easy 14-35

chorizo, tomato and chilli 21

courgette, mint and jamón 26

crab, Oloroso sherry and alioli 30

goat's cheese and roasted red onions 32

pepper, anchovy and chopped egg 18

pork, green pepper and jamón 33

steak, red wine and onions 35

tomato and jamón 22

tomato, avocado and anchovy 21

tortilla, green pepper and alioli 24-5

tomatoes: artichoke salsa with olives, capers and sun-dried tomatoes 102

baked spiced rice with tomato, prawns and green chilli 263

chopped salad 94

chorizo, tomato and chilli toast 21

eggs with chorizo, tomato and green chilli 41

ful medames 142

labneh, courgette, tomato and mint 64

labneh, sun-dried tomato, coriander and fennel seeds 57

labneh, tomato, cucumber and za'atar 61

leek, pepper and walnut bulgur pilaf 153

mackerel with tomato, olive and sherry vinaigrette 210

marinated feta, cherry tomatoes and olives 72

potato, cauliflower and squash with tomato and green chilli 252

roasted aubergines, tomatoes and tahini 108

shakshuka with green chilli and coriander salsa 44-7

spiced labneh, tomatoes, mint and dukkah 68

spinach and chickpeas 162

squid and tomato salad with crispy capers 181

tomato and jamón toast 22

tomato, avocado and anchovy toast 21

tomato bulgur with lamb and cinnamon yoghurt 271

Turkish eggs with spinach, tomato, feta and dill 48

whole roast turbot with garlic, rosemary and cherry tomatoes 261

tortilla, green pepper and alioli toast 24-5

tuna with fennel seeds, oregano and chilli 212

turbot: turbot with anchovy, rosemary and paprika butter 204

whole roast turbot with garlic, rosemary and cherry tomatoes 261

Turkish eggs with spinach, tomato, feta and dill 48

V

veal escalopes, rosemary and jamón 233

vegetables 100-39

lamb with spring vegetables 268

roast vegetables with orzo and olives 250

see also individual types of vegetable

W

walnuts: coffee, walnut and cardamom muffins 281

duck breasts with walnut and pomegranate sauce 226

erişte with leeks, yoghurt and walnuts 160

leek, pepper and walnut bulgur pilaf 153

red lentil, pepper and walnut salad with tarragon 98-9

sea bass baked with fig leaves and walnut sauce 205

watermelon, cos and feta salad 92

wine: clams, white wine and asparagus 197

clams, white wine and coriander 194

scallops with Albariño wine 198

squid, potatoes, red wine and rosemary 182

steak, red wine and onion toast 35

Y

yoghurt: cacık 114

erişte with leeks, yoghurt and walnuts 160

fried eggs with yoghurt and chilli butter 38

mussels with yoghurt, dill and crispy chickpeas 190

raspberry and yoghurt fool 286

red lentil soup with yoghurt and mint 150

roast squash, peppers, chickpeas and herby yoghurt 249

roasted aubergines, tomatoes and tahini 108

tomato bulgur with lamb and cinnamon yoghurt 271

yoghurt cheesecake with muscatel strawberries 298

Z

za'atar: boiled artichokes with za'atar 105

fried potatoes with za'atar, peppers and feta 137

labneh, tomato, cucumber and za'atar 61

about the authors

Sam and Sam Clark are the successful husband-and-wife team behind Moro.

Having spent their honeymoon exploring the flavours of Spain and Morocco, they opened Moro in Clerkenwell, London, in 1997. Since then the restaurant has enjoyed unequalled reviews and accolades, and the Clarks have opened Morito, an intimate tapas bar, with branches in Clerkenwell and Hackney.

They live in Highbury, North London, and have three children.